Suspects & Sleuth's Murder Mystery Design Guide

By: Brianna Carlisle & Steve French

TABLE OF CONTENTS

CHARTS

0. INTRODUCTION

What is a Murder Mystery Party?

A murder mystery dinner party game is an interactive live action role-playing game where your guests take on the roles of suspects or sleuth's and attempt to solve a murder. The host decorates their home to represent the scene of the crime and the guests attend dressed in costumes playing the parts of their characters. A murder will occur and the guests will try to identify the villain by investigating evidence, examining clues, and questioning each other until they can come to a conclusion. Murder mystery games are a great way to liven up your next dinner party and offer your guests an experience that they will rant and rave about for months to come.

Sure, those store bought murder mystery game kits can be quite fun, but there are a number of issues with them:

1. You may not be able to find a kit that contains the theme or genre you desire for the game you have in mind.
2. These types of games are only playable once. If you intend to play murder mystery games within the same circle of family and friends you would have to buy a new kit every time.
3. Indeed, you may buy a game kit only to find out it's game structure does not suit the needs of the play style you had in mind. The difficulty level of such a game may be too hard or not challenging enough.
4. Other writers and creators of these kits do not know you and your players. What if you do not like the characters included or more importantly your players do not like them? What if you need a scenario for all male or all female characters?
5. Developers often do not know your personal preferences. The content and themes involved in the plot of those kits may not be suitable for all of your guests.
6. Most game kits are typically dependant on a set number of players to work. They may require more players than you desire or simply not enough.
7. Additionally, they can be quite expensive.

Writing your own murder mystery game scenario is the best solution to all of those problems.

Sure, you could read a few articles on the web and gather some general information on how to write a murder mystery game. There are also a few books on the market that claim to tell you how to write these types of games, but the content is usually quite limited. Perhaps you could read one of these books, follow the instructions, and someday, after weeks of research and hard work writing, finally end up with a workable murder mystery game scenario.

What are you to do, however, when your friends and family are asking you, or begging you, to create another game and you feel your inspiration has already been spent writing the first? Where do you get more ideas and inspiration when you feel your murder mystery Muse has left the building?

Using this guide and my system is the best solution to all of these issues described. Here is why:

1. You get to decide on any time period, theme, genre, and whatever location you desire.

2. The games you create with this system are playable one time, but you can use the system to create an unique murder mystery scenario every time you desire with a new theme, new location, new event, new victim, new villain, new suspects, new clues, new plots, etc.

3. Not only can you decide on the structure of the game scenarios created with this system, but you can also customize them to meet the needs of the game style you wish to play. I will give you several variants for the games created with my system and various ideas on how to begin and end them. You can also control the level of difficulty in your scenarios.

4. Using this guide and my unique system, you have the flexibility to write characters for your game scenarios that will also suit the interests of your players, as you know them better than anyone else. You can write your scenario for all women or all men, or a combination of both.

5. My system allows you to choose whatever themes and content you feel is suitable to the type of scenario you wish to write for your players.

6. With my system and method you can write your scenarios for as many players as you might want. You can write them for six players, or one hundred. It's up to you.

7. Creating a new scenario is free, you only have to buy my book one time. You can create an endless number of scenarios with this guide using this system.

8. This guide contains numerous lists to provide you with an limitless supply of ideas and inspiration for writing a new scenario any time you want. My system is flexible and customizable. Each chart lists numerous possibilities to choose from and you are able to expand them as needed or desired.

9. I have provided all the information, suggestions, and advice you could possibly need in order to host your game event from beginning to end.

10. I include ideas for creating your own props, decorations, and costumes to be used in the game and information on how to create any game components you may need for a game. I also give you the ideas on how to achieve all this on a shoestring budget. You can make your games as cheap or as expensive and elaborate as you so desire.

In this guide you will find everything you need to create a super fabulous murder mystery.

Dear Reader, my name is Brianna Carlisle, and I enjoy hosting murder mystery dinner party games. Since you are reading this, I can make a fair guess that you might have an interest in not only writing a murder mystery game, but hosting one as well. With this book, not only will I show you how to write a murder mystery scenario, but also how to host it and how to play it from beginning to end. Whether you are a beginner, an amateur, or even an experienced writer, this book is the perfect guide for writing the professional quality, murder mystery dinner party games of your dreams.

1. USING THE SYSTEM AND CHARTS

The charts set up in this guide can be used in two different ways. It is entirely up to you which method or approach you wish to use to generate the ideas and information for your murder mystery scenario.

Option#1: You could read the lists or charts and simply select the ideas or information, as you go, which inspire you or fit the scenario you have in mind. You are never limited to the included charts or lists, they are merely provided as a starting point for further research if such a list does not encompass all the possibilities that you may require for your story. You can expand on any list as you may require to suit your needs. Every attempt has been made to include as many ideas and as much information about every aspect of a standard murder mystery game as possible.

Option#2: The charts and lists are also set up in a way that you could use polyhedral gaming dice or an online random number generator to select an idea for you, if there should come an instance where you desire a random result. The polyhedral dice you would need are: a standard 6 sided die (D6), a 10 sided die (D10), a 12 sided die (D12), and a 20 sided die (D20). If you do use dice to randomly generate ideas, never feel completely obliged to use the results if they do not work for your story, either roll again or select the appropriate idea that you need to make your story work out the way you want it to. Dice are NOT used or needed to play the games themselves.

In most cases, Option #1 may work the best for your needs, however, I use dice many times during the creation of my scenarios because I personally like the challenge of linking the random ideas together and often find that the story develops itself in rather interesting ways that may not normally occur to me. Whichever method you choose, use your imagination, creativity, and have fun with it. Ready to get started?

Note: In this guide the terms 'Moderator', 'Story Teller', or 'Referee' will be used to refer to the Host, the 'Host' being the writer, director, and the person running the game for the players.

2. MURDER MYSTERY WRITING BASICS

The first question is: Where to begin? Well, let's get started with the basics.

The basic structure of any story requires three essential stages. It must have a beginning, a middle, and an end. It's a very simple concept to follow. Although we are not writing a murder mystery novel (or maybe you are), the scenario we write for the murder mystery game, will require those three stages. It must begin somehow, it must end somehow, and there must also be a middle to tie the two together logically.

A great deal of the beginning part of the story will be played out and told by the guests, so all we really will need to do is write an introduction which will set the mood, introduce the characters, and set the scene for the scenario which will be played out. So, other than the introduction all we would need to do is write some objectives for those characters to perform so that the scenario story will unfold the way that we want it to.

We really won't have much writing to do for the middle part of the story either, because that is where all the live action role-playing happens and the story is told by the guests who play the suspects and/or sleuth's. Once again, there will be some writing involved so far as assigning the objectives, actions, and dialogue that the characters must deliver in order to continue the story. We won't have to worry about the middle part of the story going astray because it is actually supposed to, and one of two things might happen, which may, or may not change, the outcome of the story, which we shall call the 'Conclusion'.

The ending we write is not so much the end, but the 'Solution', because the players themselves will actually determine what transpires towards the near ending and conclusion of the scenario. The solution, however, will be the finale to the story and reveal the true ending of the mystery.

To create the general premise of the scenario, we will need to create the essential components of the story. We will need a victim, a villain, clues, red herrings, some suspects, perhaps some sleuth's, and finally a plot to tie everything together.

Before we get ahead of ourselves, here is some advice you should consider before getting really involved writing the scenario for your game.

First of all, when writing your scenario, you should use a word processor of some type so that you may make changes and edits easily. Writing some notes on paper is fine, but you will want to write the bulk of your story in a method that can be easily edited whenever needed.

Give yourself plenty of time to write up your mystery game scenario before announcing your game night. The first time you write a scenario it may take some time. Maybe a week, more or less, depending on how much free time you have to devote to such a project. Do not dismay, the more of these you create, the faster you will be able to write them and put a game together. With some experience you could probably get a game scenario written in a matter of a few days. Of course, the more detailed and elaborate you want your story to be, the longer it will take to write.

What you can also do, to save a lot of time when writing your next murder mystery, is to reuse the same characters. Just change their occupations if needed, change who the villain will be, change who the liar will be, create a new victim, and write your new scenario around that. You would also want to have new clues, motives, etc. You could use a new event and/or a new location, but the same location would be fine as well, if you so desire.

Some writers prefer to write up entire scripts for each of their characters to read during certain parts of the game. Do keep in mind, if you decide to use scripts, that you may deprive players and the story a certain amount of spontaneity to occur. Scripts can put a lot of limitations on what your players can think and do of their own accord. Allowing player spontaneity can inspire some really memorable moments in your games. Try to let your players be creative with their characters actions and thoughts during your event.

If you are using this system to write a Murder Mystery Play, then by all means write the scripts you want or need, otherwise try to avoid too much scripting.

For a standard murder mystery party you want an interactive murder mystery game, not a series of scripted events. It is up to you, but just remember that the more work you make for your players the longer your game will take to play. If everyone has the time, that is perfectly acceptable. Keep in mind how long you want to play a game before writing too many details into your story.

Now, before we get started on plot and characters, we will want to know a few things about the general scenario. We will need a theme, location, and a premise for the murder mystery. Lets answer the following standard questions that every writer must answer when creating a story outline: The Who, What, Where, When, How, and Whys. Be sure to start taking notes now, if you like, and begin creating your very first murder mystery scenario.

3. THEMES AND GENRE

Let us first select a theme or genre, which is usually a certain time period in which the scenario will take place. You can use any of these you like as it suits your needs, or you can randomly select one using dice. In the example I shall demonstrate, I have decided for a 1920's theme throughout the duration of this guide, but as I said before, this system is not limited to any set specifics. Using the following chart, you can choose a theme which will set the overall mood and atmosphere for your murder mystery.

Chart#1 Theme (Common themes used in many Murder Mystery Games)

D20

1. The roaring 1920's! -Flappers, Jazz and silent film nostalgia.
2. 1950's -Hard Boiled Detective Nostalgia.
3. Pirates -Plunder, Galleons, and Pieces of Eight.
4. Western -Frontier Justice, Saloons and Gunslinger's.
5. Modern Day -Anywhere and Anyhow.
6. Science Fiction -Futuristic, Distant Planets and Spaceships.
7. Renaissance -Medieval mayhem.
8. 1940's -War Era and Big Band Nostalgia.
9. 1970's -Peace, love, and Disco.
10. 1980's -Retro, Rock and Pop culture.
11. 1960's -Cars, Diners, Dame's, and Derbies.
12. Cloak and Dagger, Spies and Intrigue. (could also be in any time period)
13. Horror -Ghosts, Vampires, Zombies...you name it. (could also be in any time period)
14. Ancient Rome. Toga party!
15. Ancient Egypt. Pharaoh's, Pyramids, Tombs, and perhaps Mummies.
16. Civil War. Blues versus Grays.
17. Napoleonic Revolution. Frock Coats and Swashbuckling.
18. Gangsters -1930's Swing Dances, Prohibition and Tommy Guns.
19. Holly Wood Celebrities. (could be any time in Hollywood movie history)
20. Holliday Specific. (could also be in any time period)

Using Chart#1 will tell me the general time period. It will also give me an idea on the characters and the atmosphere I will want to write for. Go ahead and decide on one that interests you now, and make a note of it. If you do not find the theme you desire from the above chart, you can use any other similar theme that would work for for your scenario.

4. LOCATION

Now we shall decide, where exactly, the scenario will take place. This chart will help you decide the physical structure or general location for the setting. This too will help us determine more atmosphere for the story. In the case of determining the location, it might be better to choose one that fits your genre, obviously some of these would not work together (for example Ancient Rome and Ski Resort) and for such cases chose a location that may not be listed here that suits your specific time period. Most of these fit locations of the 20th century.

Chart#2 Location (common locations in Murder Mystery Games)

D20
1. Cruise Ship / River Boat / Paddle Wheel Steam Boat / Submarine / War Ship
2. Vegas Casino / Gambling Hall / Saloon
3. Mysterious Mansion / Manor / House / Castle
4. Country Inn / Bed and Breakfast / Ranch
5. Passenger Train / Airplane / Bus
6. Theater: Opera, Musical, Play, Movie
7. Resort / Vacation Resort / Tropical Island
8. Museum / Library / Art Exhibit
9. Night Club / Bar / Speakeasy/ Burlesque Club/ Tavern / Pub / Jazz Lounge
10. Church / Cathedral / Abbey
11. High School / College / Educational Institute / School
12. Hospital / Asylum
13. Private Yacht / Galleon / Sloop
14. Cabin in the Woods / Camp Ground
15. Hotel / Motel
16. Office Building
17. Restaurant / Diner / Coffee House
18. Country Club / Private Club
19. Ski Lodge / Ski Resort
20. Light House

Using the chart above, I decided a Mysterious Manor, although somewhat cliche, would make an excellent location for my 1920's Murder Mystery example. I will use this example in this guide to help you understand how I will put all of this information together to make a coherent murder mystery game story, complete with plot.

Note that many of the locations, on the previous page, could really make great atmosphere for any murder mystery scenario. Imagine, for a moment, how exciting it would be, to be involved in solving a murder mystery in the 1950's, on a River Boat in New Orleans, Louisiana.

The next chart is for determining where in the world you might want your murder mystery to take place. Keep in mind, this is a general list of ideas to help inspire you, there are hundreds or more great and exotic locations in the world where you could place the geographical setting for your scenario. Either select from the following list or determine a geographical location by research that fits your over all theme.

Chart# 2b Where in the World?

Western Hemisphere		Eastern Hemisphere	
1.	Alaska	1.	Africa
2.	Greenland	2.	Iceland
3.	The Bahamas	3.	Spain
4.	Canada	4.	France
5.	United States	5.	Germany
6.	Mexico	6.	Italy
7.	Central America	7.	Poland
8.	Cuba	8.	Turkey
9.	Haiti	9.	Denmark
10.	Dominican Republic	10.	Sweden
11.	Caribbean Islands	11.	Greece
12.	Hawaii	12.	Morocco
13.	Venezuela	13.	India
14.	Ecuador	14.	Russia
15.	Peru	15.	China
16.	Bolivia	16.	Japan
17.	Chile	17.	Singapore
18.	Argentina	18.	United Kingdom
19.	Brazil	19.	Australia
20.	Colombia	20.	New Zealand

5. SCENARIO EVENT

Once we have a theme and general location for the story, we need an idea about why all of the suspects will have to come together and to be present when the murder occurs. Determining this information also helps to add some suspension of disbelief and atmosphere for the story line. The following chart entails common, classic events, often used in murder mystery games and stories. You may choose one randomly or pick one that pique's your interest and inspires you.

Chart #3 Scenario Event

D20

1. Wedding Reception / Marriage Ceremony
2. Graduation (High School/ College/ Military) Celebration Party
3. Family Reunion / Banquet / Picnic / BBQ / Hawaii style Luau Party
4. Wake / Funeral / Reading the Will
5. Birthday Party / Bar mitzvah etc.
6. Holliday Gathering (any Holliday you can think of should work)
7. Celebration Party (Movie Premiers / Job Promotions) / Party
8. Business Dinner Meeting
9. Costume Party / Ball Masque / Masquerade Ball / Dance Party
10. Awards Ceremony (Movies / Music / Arts / TV)
11. Tournament (Pool / Poker / Sports)
12. Contest or Auction
13. Class Reunion
14. Festival / Mardi Gras / State Fare / Parade / Circus
15. Homecoming Dance or Prom
16. Convention (Themes like Comics, Games, Movies ,Wine Tasting, etc.)
17. Vacation Trip (Could be anywhere you want it to be)
18. Concert (Rock / Symphony / Opera)
19. Bridal Shower / Baby Shower / Bachelor Party
20. Beauty Pageant / Fashion Show

Using Chart #3, I determined a Celebration Party of some type would suit the story just fine for what I have in mind so far. Once again, some of these might not work with your time period so, just choose a similar event for your genre that would make sense.

Most of these events can be tweaked to your genre with a little imagination. For example, if you had chosen a Medieval theme, the location were a Castle somewhere in England, and you choose a Contest or Auction event, perhaps this would be a Jousting Tournament, or some type of competitive game like an Archery contest, or something similar.

6. CREATING CHARACTERS

It is now time to start working on the characters for the scenario. The first character we will need is a victim. I already know it is the 1920's, we are at an old Manor, and someone is having a celebration party. I might even go so far as to decide that the Manor is located in Manitou Springs, Colorado. Before we can create a victim or any suspects, we will need to come up with a simple method for establishing gender, names, ages, and even a little bit of personality for the characters in the story. This chapter is divided into several sub-chapters that can be used later for reference, because these charts can be used again to gather information about all of the characters.

6a. Naming Characters

The victim must have a name, and so will the suspects. Here are some simple ideas on how to come up with names for your characters.

Before you choose a name, we need to know the gender of the victim or suspect. You could flip a coin to decide or just choose one based upon any ideas you may have swimming through your head at this exact moment. However, when we do get around to making the suspects list, we will try to balance the ratio of males to females, unless of course, you wish your scenario written for all men, or all women, or any combination thereof.

You could buy a 'Baby Names' book, but there are free ways to do this also. You probably have two dust covered phone books in your home, one outside by the front door, and one hanging in a plastic bag on the fence -I know I do. Phone books are full of names, pick a first and last name for your characters at random.

Another suggestion is to use the Internet to find names for your characters, there are many free sites for finding names from many nationalities and historical time periods. There are also sites that can randomly create character names for you. I typically use a naming site, however, and choose names for my characters that sound interesting.

Some writers of murder mystery games give their characters rather outlandish or down right silly names for their characters, involving a play on words or perhaps a pun. An example would be a female character named 'Miss Demeanor' or a male character named 'Mister E. Saulvor'. It is up to you how you want to name your characters, whichever method you choose is fine.

6b. Determining the Age of Characters

You can decide an age for your characters or determine the information randomly. Your characters could be young from 20-39, middle aged from 40-59, or elderly 60-79. It all will depend on how you see the character in question in your imagination.

Here is a simple formula I use to randomly determine an age for my characters, if I cant decide on one. Using a D6, and a D10, I will be able to generate an age range from 10 to 69, but I don't like children or teens to be victims of a crime, so I will add 10 to the result so that my characters will range from 20 to 79. That being said we don't have to kill any overly elderly characters either. Using the D6, I rolled a 2, and on the D10, I rolled a 4, but I don't add the results, instead it gives me the two numbers I need, which results in 24, and then I add the 10 to end up with 34. So far I have determined the name, gender and age of my victim. I now introduce you to Colby Brenton, Male, age 34 years old.

6c. Character Personalities

Creating some memorable personalities for the characters should be easy enough if we avoid becoming to complex in the decision making process. Here are a few useful tips and tricks that we can use for the 'Acting Advice' part of the character dossiers which we shall create later in the game. We can also use the following methods to set up personalities to non-suspect characters, including the victim.

Part of how we describe a characters persona could be based on the characters particular occupation. We want the characters to either be comedic, stereotypical, over the top, or larger than life. This will make them memorable, a lot of fun to play, and rather easy to play.

Some murder mystery writers may wish to take their characters development even further than that, and that is fine, it is all up to you. If you wish to do that, here is an really easy way to assign some general personality traits to each character. What we can do is give them a Birth Sign. Each of the twelve zodiac signs describe a certain number of personality features. Just pick a Birth Sign and then look it up on the Internet. Choose three positive traits and three negative traits for the character based on their sign. Just be sure to give the character a Birth Sign that will not be the exact same as that of their own real life sign or perhaps there will be no challenge in the role.

7. THE VICTIM

Now we are ready to create details for the most important person in the murder mystery scenario. Someone must now be killed in a devious manner, otherwise, there is no crime for the players to solve. I will guess the person getting killed is the host of this party, a resident of the manor, and that might become very relevant to the story as it develops. There are a number of things we need to get to know about this victim or they will be a boring cardboard character. If you have not done so already, first decide the victims gender, name, age, and, if you desire, a general personality based on the methods described in Chapter 6. After that is done, we will want to know the victims occupation, and the details involving his or her untimely death.

7a. Victim Occupation

Colby Brenton needs an occupation to give us some insight into his character. I will use the chart on the next page to do this, but you can create your own if you like. Note that this chart is only used for determining the victims occupation, we will use slightly different charts for the suspects and I will explain why later. The reason I have a separate occupation chart for the victim is because I want the players to feel empathy, pity, or even disdain for the victim in question. I think you will understand what I mean as you select your victims occupation.

This next chart lists occupation based on gender, with a male and a female alternative, but feel free to ignore and challenge gender boundaries. This chart was made to reflect occupations common in the 20th century, but you can customize one to reflect your genre and/or time period if necessary, or use an equivalent. As you will see, a lot of the occupations I listed would make for some really interesting high-profile murder mystery cases. If you can not find what you need here, you should be able to do some online research, and find an occupation that suits the needs for your particular victim and genre.

Chart#4 Victim Occupation (common victim occupations used in murder mysteries)

Roll D20	MALE	FEMALE
1)	Accountant	Rich Widow or Heiress
2)	Police Detective	Ambassador
3)	Stock Broker	Antique Dealer
4)	Business Owner	Shop Keeper
5)	Gangster (crook)	Attorney
6)	Bookie	Call Girl
7)	Gambler	Editor or Reporter
8)	Con Man	Photographer / Photo Journalist
9)	Politician	Actress / Film star
10)	Lawyer	Physician / Therapist
11)	Political Activist	Governor / Mayor
12)	Rich Play Boy	Student / Intern
13)	Federal Agent	Museum Curator
14)	Judge	Madame
15)	Minister/Priest	Cocktail Waitress
16)	Spy	Burlesque Dancer
17)	Sports Star	Socialite / Flapper
18)	Bartender	Night Club Singer
19)	Musician	Secretary / Clerk
20)	Chef / Cook	Maid / House Keeper / Nanny

Using the chart above to determine Colby's occupation, I rolled the D20, and hit 19, which will make him a musician of some sort. I decide he's a Jazz musician, maybe plays Saxophone. Who would want to murder the Jazz musician? We will find that out a little later. There is much more I will want to know about Colby Brenton, but as the rest of the information is generated I will probably learn a lot more about him in the process. For now we should move on to the next step and figure out how the victim will be murdered.

7b. Determining the Cause of Death

There are many ways a person could die, but this is murder, we want to narrow down the possibilities to methods common in murder mystery stories. We should choose a cause of death that the suspects and/or sleuth's can determine when examining the body. You could have a murder mystery involving an automobile hit and run, or other such tragedy if you wish, but here are the ones that I think will work best for this type of game.

Chart#5 Cause of Death

D6

1. Blunt Trauma: Caused by bludgeoning with a blunt object such as a club, crowbar, tire-iron, a candlestick, a lead pipe, wrench, baseball bat, marble ashtray, pool ball, etc.
2. Stabbing / Slashing: Knife, Dagger, sharp object, etc.
3. Gunshot: Revolver, Pistol, Handgun, Rifle, etc.
4. Strangulation / Asphyxiation: Using a rope, belt, a wire cord, etc.
5. Suffocation: Smothering using a pillow, or similar method/weapon.
6. Poisoning: Arsenic, Cyanide, Belladonna, Chloroform -to name a few.

You could add drowning to the list, or any other method for murder, so long as you can provide a reasonable way for the suspects to determine the cause of death, and link such evidence to a suspect, or suspects. The list above reflects common methods of murder fairly easy to link to some type of weapon which could eventually be linked to one or more suspects.

Using the chart above, I rolled a D6, which resulted in a 5, meaning Colby was smothered to death -probably with a pillow. Knowing this, I now have a weapon for the murder, although not a very sinister one in this case.

Note: Be cautious when writing the use of poisons as a method of murder in your story. There are a number of ways poison could be delivered long before it would take effect, giving the killer time to cover their tracks, and create an elaborately clever alibi. If it is delivered by food or drink, the question would become: When did the victim actually ingest the poison and how long did it take to kill them? Using poison as a method for murder in this way is perfectly fine, so long as you are ready to do some research and find a way for the killer to eventually be identified. You would also have to devise a way to link the other suspects to have access to the poison as well, otherwise it becomes too obvious who the killer could be. Perhaps the easiest way is to suggest that the murderer would have used a syringe to inject and deliver a poisonous or toxic substance into the victim, which is almost immediately fatal.

7c. Time of Death

Time of death is usually an important piece of information, which suspects and sleuth's may use to find out who was where at the time of the crime, and to perhaps shed light on who has an opportunity to commit the murder and who may have a legitimate alibi.

You don't have to randomly determine this, just pick a time that works for your story, but if you should need to determine a time randomly, here is the method I sometimes use.

Using the face of a clock for reference, I can use a D12 to determine a rough estimate for the hour and minutes for the time of death. Here is an example of the formula: I roll the D12, which results in 12. Then I roll the D12 again, which results in a 9. The first roll determined where the hour hand of the clock would be pointing, thus 12, and the second roll determined the position of the minute hand at 9, thus 45 minutes after 12. We don't need to be any more exact than that for a murder mystery game. There is one last question I need to answer here: Was it A.M. or P.M.? Flip a coin if you like. Heads for AM and Tails for PM. Doing that, I find out Colby Benton was killed at about 12:45 AM, which is in the morning, just after the Witching Hour.

7d. Place of Body & Scene of the Crime

Now we will want to know where the body was eventually found, which may or may not be the actual crime scene. To determine this I need to refer to the location I chose for my scenario, in this case, an old manor. I can guess what kind of rooms may be present in such an old house. You will have to make a list of rooms and locations relevant to the place of your story. Use your imagination, or visit a place similar to the one you will use in your story. You may be able to find maps online of similar places, and make such a list. You could randomly determine the exact location, or chose one that works for your story. As an example, on the following page, is a list of rooms I made for my old manor.

1. Parlor
2. Lounge
3. Billiards Room
4. Kitchen
5. Dining Room
6. Pantry
7. Conservatory
8. Study
9. Library
10. Bedroom
11. Guest Bedroom
12. Master Bedroom
13. Bathroom
14. Garden
15. Patio
16. Carriage House
17. Foyer
18. Attic
19. Basement
20. Observatory

I was able to list twenty different rooms to choose from, but I could not make up my mind which room to use. In this case, I used a D20 to determine a room for me. I rolled a 3, which means Colby Brenton's body was found in the Billiards Room. A strange place to be killed with a pillow no doubt, which brings me to my next question. Is this the scene of the crime? Where the body is found, is not necessarily where the crime was committed.

It is really up to you how you wish to handle the game scenario as far as the actual crime scene, and the location of the body when it is discovered. Having two areas for sleuth's or suspects to investigate does help the method of the game, because the clues should be discovered over the course of a few stages.

Typically, in a murder mystery game, the players are never given all of the clues at one time, instead, they need to find a few at a time, which may help them narrow down the list of possible suspects, and or to gradually better understand the circumstances of the crime that was committed.

If you decide that the crime scene and the location where the body is discovered are to be one and the same, then you should place half your legitimate clues and half your red herrings here. Have a secondary location to hide the rest of the clues and red herrings. Alternatively, you could hide these remaining clues and red herrings all over the place and have the players perform a 'Treasure Hunt' style game in order to discover them.

If the crime scene and the location where the body is discovered are to be separate places, than it is a simple matter of placing some clues and red herrings with the body. The remaining clues and red herrings should be placed at the actual crime scene.

In the case of the my scenario, I have decided that the body of Colby Brenton will be found in the Billiards Room, but he was actually killed somewhere else. I could randomly determine the real scene of the crime using the list I made, but since Colby was killed with a pillow, I decide he was actually killed in his bedroom. The scenario is starting to become clearer and the story line is just now starting to write it'self based on some random rolls and logical decisions.

Basically, what we are doing so far is, we are building the scenario, starting with the victim, and slowly writing the structure of the mystery around the details pertaining to the murder. It is done in this way so that we can later, as the scenario develops and the details of the crime become clear, make logical decisions regarding what suspects will be needed and what details we should add to the final plot of the story itself. It is better to do it in this way than to write a handful of characters first, decide which one gets killed, then decide which one is the murderer, etc. If you were to do it in that method, while fleshing out the details of the plot, you may later find that some of your characters are not going to work out for the scenario that you at first had in mind and that perhaps even the clues you were going to use will not fit the mystery aspect of the game.

Here are the victim notes for Colby Brenton so far.

<u>Murder at Brenton Manor</u>

Victim Notes

Victim: Colby Brenton, Male, 34yrs old.

Occupation: Amateur Jazz Musician, Sax player

Marital Status: ???

Family: ???

In-laws: ???

Employees: ???

Finances: ???

Secrets: ???

Friends: ???

Acquaintances: ???

Hobbies: ???

Habits: ???

Political Affiliations: ???

Religion: ???

Cause of Death: Suffocation / Asphyxiation by Pillow

Time of Death: 12:45 AM -8/11/1922

Place of Body: Billiard Room

Scene of Crime: Colby's Bedroom

Notice there are still some unanswered questions about Colby Brenton's personal life, but once again, I will let the story develop on its own while creating the other details of the mystery. Once I have created the other suspects I can probably fill in the blanks above with some more interesting information.

8. CLUES AND EVIDENCE

We still need some suspects for the mystery, but before I choose my suspects, I need to know what clues are going to be found first. Reason being, I will need to pin clues and red herrings on the suspects to link them to the crime. I also want to be able to select suspects who can evaluate the clues found at the scene of the crime, and I will show you how to do that a bit later. Lets generate some clues to be found. For every murder I want to choose or randomly generate at least four incriminating clues, and at least four false clues or red herrings.

The following chart lists several types of clues that are often found in real crime scenes which are often used in murder mystery novels as plot devices. There are probably a dozen or more clues that could be added, such as broken glass, paint chips, food crumbs, physical markings, etc. So, expand if necessary, or select the clues that you feel are important to your particular story.

Chart#6 CLUES

D20

1. Dust
2. Dirt / Soil
3. Bullet / or broken piece of the weapon
4. Gunshot Residue
5. Carpet Fiber / Rug Fiber
6. Typed Note (Legal Document, Business Card, Letter, Receipt, etc.)
7. Ashes* (could be from a cigarette, pipe, cigar or even from a hearth)
8. Shoe Print / Foot Impression / Shoe Polish Smudge
9. Cloth Fiber Sample (can be matched to someone's clothing perhaps)
10. Handwritten Note (Love Note / Dear John / Threat / Warning)
11. Weapon* (type will depend on method of murder or cause of death)
12. Finger Print / Hand Print
13. Hair Sample (could also be a toupee or wig sample)
14. Blood Sample (either the victims or a suspects)
15. Lipstick Smudge (or make-up of some type)
16. Cigarette butt or Cigar stump (Smoking Pipe / Snuff / Chew, etc.)
17. Plant Fibers / Pollen Sample / Leaves / Flower / Herb
18. Personal Item (see chart# 6a -next page)
19. Wound / Teeth Marks / Scratches / Bruise (bite marks either on victim or a suspect)
20. Puzzle Clue (see Chapter 8a Puzzle Clues)

Chart#6a Personal Item

D12

1. Key (House Key, Room Key, Hotel Key, Car Key, Deposit Box Key, Key to a Safe)
2. Piece of Jewelry (Pin, Buckle, Watch, Ring, Necklace, Earring, Cufflink, Gem, etc.)
3. Piece of Clothing (Hat, Glove, Shoelace, Button, Scarf, Handkerchief, Tie, etc.)
4. Rare Coin (One of the suspects may be a Coin Collector for example.)
5. Photograph (could be a picture of almost anything)
6. Drawing (Sketch/ Map / Plans)
7. Cosmetic Item (Chapstick, Perfume, Lipstick, Eye-Shadow, Powder Case, Mirror, etc.)
8. Eye-Glasses (Sunglasses, Monocle, Spectacles, etc.)
9. Comb / Hairbrush (Mustache Comb or similar grooming item)
10. Pill Bottle (medication / drug)
11. Good Luck Charm (Rabbits Foot, Rock or Stone, Figurine, Dice, Trinket, etc.)
12. Writing Pen (could be unique to a particular individual)

Using Chart#6, I rolled four times using a D20 and generated the following valid clues that will be found at the scene of the crime or at the location where the body is to be discovered.

Teeth Marks

Ashes

Gunshot Residue

Lipstick Smudge

There was a problem, however, with the gunshot residue clue. Colby was murdered with a pillow. I cant link gunshot residue to the villain in this case, but instead of erasing it and re-rolling a new clue, I decide it might be relevant to the story later. At this point it does not make sense to me that the villain would have gunshot residue on their hands, since the weapon used was a pillow. So, I decide the residue is on the victims hand. This means he fired a weapon recently, perhaps a revolver. Did he try to defend himself by taking a shot at the villain? If so, this could turn out to be valid evidence later.

Now I have to add a revolver to the clues and I need to know where the discharged bullet went. It cant be in the villains body otherwise the suspects and/or sleuth's can easily identify the murderer. Whoever has been shot did it. That won't work, so I will say Colby missed.

Using some classical detective style deduction I can probably determine where the bullet is.

Colby was in his bedroom at 12:45 AM when he was murdered with a pillow. That means the villain was most likely on top of him, suffocating him with the pillow, when Colby reached for the revolver which he keeps near his bed. He must be a bit paranoid, or have some good reason to keep a revolver so handy, and maybe I will add that to the story. Colby attempts to shoot the assailant, but his final moment has come. He passes out, but manages to shoot off a round of the revolver. If he was trying to shoot the villain, he was probably trying to aim at them, but we know he missed the villain straddling him, thus he would have shot a bullet into the ceiling of his bedroom. This turns out to be valuable information that the players must figure out somehow during the course of the investigation, reason being is that the bullet hole in the ceiling will prove where the murder was actually committed, and reveals the true scene of the crime.

I will also have to note that in Colby's bedroom, there will be a revolver laying on the floor, near or on the bed. More evidence. I can hide some of the above mentioned clues here and possibly some red herrings. Now the list of valid clues becomes:

Teeth Marks -?

Ashes -somewhere in Colby's bedroom.

Gunshot Residue -on hand of the victim.

Lipstick smudge -on victim's shirt collar.

Revolver -on the floor in Colby's bedroom.

Bullet Hole -in the Ceiling of Colby's bedroom.

Pillow -weapon, found near the bed.

Note that I am still not sure about how to fit in the teeth marks as a clue yet, so I will come back to it later, towards the end of the story.

8a. Puzzle Clues

What is a Puzzle Clue? Well, for one thing, it's not typically the kind of clue you would find at an actual real life crime scene. In a murder mystery game, however, you could use these as little mini-mysteries that would need to be solved by the players in order for them to gain certain information, or to find, or evaluate another clue that might be needed for the game.

There are several types of puzzle clues that could be used in this type of game. Anagrams, brain teaser's, logic puzzles, math puzzles, cryptograms, riddles, and visualization puzzles would all be great examples. Here are some puzzle ideas you could use.

In the case of the 'Handwritten Letter' clue, perhaps, the important contents of the letter have been written in lemon juice with a toothpick. This message would not be visible. At the bottom of the letter, written in pen, it could say, 'only light can reveal the hidden'. You would have to make this secret message yourself, and the players would have to figure out the meaning of the cryptic message written on the letter. By holding up the letter to a lamp they would be able to read the hidden message itself, which could be information or a clue.

Another way you could write a secret letter is with a white wax candle or a crayon on white paper. It would be hard to read unless it is painted over with watercolors. The paint would not stick to the portions written in wax. Perhaps a cryptic message written in pen at the bottom of the message reads, 'paint me'.

You can also buy special pens that write in a clear ink, but the message shows up under a black light. You can also look up a recipe for 'Disappearing Ink' on the Internet, a message written in this way will disappear as it dries, but rubbing over the message with a cotton ball dipped in ammonia will make the hidden message return.

Perhaps a letter found is a riddle of sorts that requires reference to a book to be solved. For example, the riddle could be:

'Curiouser and curiouser!' C2: 4x5=?

The quote refers to something Alice would say in 'Alice in Wonderland', the C2 would refer to Chapter Two, 'The Pool of Tears', where at some point Alice starts quoting mathematical equations followed by a wrong answer. In this case, Alice says 'four times five is twelve', thus the answer to the riddle is 12. The players would need access to the 'Alice in Wonderland' story in order to find the answer. The book should be laying somewhere nearby where they could find it. Once the players have found and announced the answer, the moderator could reward them with a tangible clue in the game. That clue could be legitimate or a red herring.

Codes, ciphers, and secret language messages are also great puzzle clues that would require a 'key' to the code to be deciphered. The players would have to find the 'code key' in order to correctly translate the message. The clue could be the revealed message itself or a hint to a location of a hidden tangible clue or red herring.

Be both clever, and creative, when using puzzles and riddles for use as clues in your murder mystery scenarios. Be sure the puzzles you use are not so hard that they would take away from the fun of the actual murder mystery game scenario itself.

9. RED HERRINGS

Among the legitimate clues in your mystery, you should also place some red herrings into the mix in order to cast suspicion on those suspects who shall be innocent. If not, the mystery will not be challenging for your players to solve. Select at least four more 'clues' from Chart#6 to serve as red herrings in your scenario and make a note of them along with your list of valid clues.

If I do not add some red herrings to the scenario, you will see that we can already determine the gender of the villain and eliminate all male suspects. The number one reason is that the lipstick smudge, on the victims collar, is a valid clue and can be traced to one female suspect. Now we know the villain is in fact a female, unless the lipstick smudge is a clue to the villains motive. In this case, I decide the lipstick smudge clue determines the murderer to be a woman. Now I should add at least four red herrings, so that I can also cast suspicion on the male suspects. Using Chart#6, I will roll the D20 four more times to determine my red herrings. The list of false clues I generated are as follows:

Hair sample

Lipstick smudge

Dust

Bullet

Interesting. There is not one, but two, lipstick smudges on the victims collar or clothing. Colby has been a busy boy, I know this because the second smudge can not be the villains, it is a false clue and must be linked to an innocent suspect. There is a minor problem though, the bullet red herring.

It will not take long for the players to discover that Colby has not been shot, so how does the bullet serve as a red herring? I ponder it for awhile and decide to throw it into the story. Perhaps the bullet belongs to the revolver that is lying on the floor next to Colby's bed. It might serve as a minor distraction, but will most likely be discarded as evidence. In this case, I decide it's a story device, but not a valid red herring or clue. So I roll one more time on Chart#6 Clues, with the D20, and find a 'Hand Written Note'. Thats much better. This handwritten note could be any type of letter that I can use to make an innocent suspect look suspicious, especially if it is a threat note. Now the red herring list is complete with:

Hair Sample

Lipstick smudge

Dust

Bullet

Handwritten Note

The total list of possible clues is, however, as follows with notes:

Teeth Marks (True)

Ashes (True)

Gunshot Residue (Irrelevant)

Lipstick Smudge (True)

Revolver (Irrelevant)

Bullet Hole in Ceiling (establishes Scene Of Crime)

Pillow (weapon)

Hair Sample (False)

Lipstick smudge #2 (False)

Dust (False)

Bullet (Irrelevant)

Handwritten Note (False)

Note that when all of the clues and red herrings are eventually gathered, the players will not know which ones are real and which ones are false, without careful examination of the evidence.

10. SUSPECTS

Now it is time to choose some suspects for your scenario. Six to eight suspects total, including the villain, are standard for a typical murder mystery game. You may need suspects for your story who can evaluate the evidence in some way. Otherwise, no one will know exactly how to use such clues to solve the case. Choose however many suspects you might need from the following charts or choose for them an occupation relevant to your particular scenario. I have included two charts here, one for male suspects and one for female suspects, listing twenty different possible occupational choices for each. In some cases, you could use the following charts to randomly select suspects, but I feel it may be more important to select them based upon their possible areas of expertise. Feel free to challenge the gender roles and assign occupations to either male or female suspects as you see fit.

Chart#7 Male Suspect Occupations and Area of Expertise

(select by need)

1. Lawyer (match handwriting samples)
2. Butcher (match blood samples, match stab wounds to sharp weapon)
3. Dentist (match tooth samples, match teeth marks to teeth)
4. Pharmacist (identify poisoning as cause of death / match poison samples)
5. Barber (match hair samples)
6. Banker (match handwriting samples)
7. Professor (match handwriting samples)
8. Butler (match dust and carpet samples)
9. Tailor (match cloth fiber samples, match clothing evidence to apparel)
10. Shoe Salesman (match shoes to impressions or prints / match shoe polish samples)
11. Journalist (match typed documents)
12. Botanist (match plant fibers / match pollen samples / match soil samples)
13. Gardener (match soil, dirt, plant fibers, pollen samples)
14. Constable (match bullets to fire arms / identify gunshot residue/ ballistics)
15. Tobacconist (match ash samples to ashes or tobacco from cigarettes, pipes, cigars)
16. Doctor (match blood samples, identify blunt trauma and match wounds to the weapon)
17. Mortician (establish time of death, cause of death, match wounds to weapon)
18. Colonel (ballistics, match bullets to guns, match wounds to bullet or firearm)
19. Surgeon (identify stab wounds / match stab wounds to sharp weapon)
20. E.R. Tech (identify asphyxiation, establish time of death, match asphyxiation to weapon)

Chart#8 Female Suspect Occupations and Expertise

(select by need)

1. Maid (match dust samples, match carpet fiber samples)
2. Florist (match pollen, dirt, soil, plant fiber samples)
3. Author/Writer (match handwritten samples and match typed documents)
4. Secretary (match typed documents)
5. Teacher (match handwriting samples)
6. Beautician /Hairstylist (match hair samples /match lipstick smudge samples)
7. Seamstress (match cloth fiber samples / match clothing items to apparel)
8. Bank Teller (match handwriting samples /signatures)
9. Starlet / Socialite (match ash samples to cigarettes/ match cosmetics samples)
10. Manager of Apparel Boutique (match clothing items to apparel)
11. Nurse (match blood samples / establish cause of death)
12. Detective (Ballistics, match bullets to guns/ match wounds to bullets/ match fingerprints)
13. Midwife / Nanny (match poison samples / identify poisoning cause of death)
14. Attorney (match handwritten or typed documents)
15. Journalist (match typed documents)
16. Librarian (match typed documents)
17. Physician (Identify time of death, cause of death, match wounds to a weapon)
18. Psychologist (judge of character?)
19. Fortune Teller (match fingerprint / handprint samples)
20. Judge (match hand written letters / match typed documents)

By reading through Charts#7 and #8 you should be able to get some ideas on the types of suspect characters you might need for your scenario. Each occupation listed on these charts comes with an area of expertise that the suspect character could use to evaluate the evidence in your scenario.

Using Charts #7 and #8, I will select eight suspects based on who can understand the particular clues and red herrings that will be found in my murder mystery scenario example. I will also try to balance the gender ratio of males to females. In this game, it appears that I would need a total of eight players to make the game work. I could add more, or remove a few if necessary, so long as I can keep the murder mystery challenging enough.

My list of suspects is not complete by any means, I need to give them names and perhaps personalities using the methods described in Chapter 6. I may also wish to establish their age.

Here is the list of the suspects I selected with notes on why I chose them.

Dentist -female   (she could shed light on the bite marks)

Tobacconist -male (he can match the ash samples)

Constable -male   (ballistics, he can evaluate evidence related to firearms)

Barber -male   (he could match the hair samples)

Beautician -female (she can match lipstick smudge samples to cosmetic brands)

Maid -female   (she can match dust samples)

Banker -male   (he can match handwriting samples)

Fortune Teller   (she could match fingerprint samples)

As you can see I am stepping a little bit into the fantastical here and bending the suspension of disbelief just a tiny bit, but perhaps you can see the allure here of having suspects who can actually double as sleuth's by using their personal areas of expertise to evaluate the clues and evidence they might discover during their investigation. The reason for this method is in case you are not going to play a Sleuth's versus Suspects style of game and you need the suspects to be able to evaluate clues and evidence.

You might be wondering how a Fortune Teller could match fingerprint samples. Fortune Tellers read palms, as you probably know, the art of this divination requires the Fortune Teller to study hand and finger prints and to associate a particular fortune in accordance to the lines on their hands. Thus, a fortune teller may have a fair chance of matching finger or hand print samples, in a fictional game of course.

Note that I also have an interesting list of suspects here, one of which is the killer, and we already have established it is one of the female suspects. It could be the Dentist, the Beautician, the Maid, or the Fortune Teller. There will also be a liar amongst them, who is not the killer, to mix things up a bit and the liar could be male or female.

After you have chosen your suspects, give them each a name, gender, an age, and a personality (if you desire), using the methods described in Chapter 6.

11. IDENTIFYING THE KILLER OR WHODUNIT?

With the list of suspects and clues complete you can now decide which of your characters will be the murderer in your scenario. You could randomly determine your murderer or pick one now that interests you. Perhaps the valid clues you determined for your story already seem to suggest someone in particular or narrows down your possible options for suspects to choose from. Sometimes, choosing a villain for your scenario is not an easy decision to make.

I usually pick my villain based on what inspiration I might have imagined while gathering the information determined thus far in the process of developing the scenario to this point. If I do not have someone particular in mind by this point, I will make a decision based on logical reasoning.

Now that I have the suspects and clues, I must determine which one of them is guilty. Once again, I must use some classical deduction to make the final decision. It could be the Dentist, but she would not be able to shed light on the bite marks during the course or conclusion of the game, because she would have to incriminate herself by doing so. I don't want her off the hook for the crime either, so I must make her a suspicious character during the story. It could be the Beautician, but once again, if she is too cooperative she will implicate herself.

This leaves a difficult decision for me between the Maid and the Fortune Teller. Out of the two, the Fortune Teller would seem to be the least likely suspect. To witty sleuth's, that could also make her seem to be a primary suspect, because she might not seem to have much to contribute to the investigation. The Maid seems to make a perfect villain, but she is also almost, too obvious a choice. In this case, I make a final decision that the murderer will be the Fortune Teller, because it seems it will be a challenge to give her a motive and fit her into the story.

You can determine the murderer for your scenario however you see fit by reason and logic.

12. MATCHING THE CLUES TO THE SUSPECTS

We know who the murderer is now, but we need to find a way for the sleuth's to match the clues to the guilty suspect. In my example scenario, the Teeth marks, Ashes, and Lipstick Smudge will point to the Fortune Teller. The red herrings will be pointed to the innocents to throw everyone off of her trail.

There are basically two different ways to match clues and red herrings to the suspects, depending on how you want your game style to be.

If you want a murder mystery scenario that will be based on a method of deduction, than here is the basic formula you will want to follow when assigning not only the physical clues, but also when writing the suspects testimonies.

The truthful testimony, the factual clues and legitimate evidence should show, if you have eight suspects, that six of eight of your suspects will have access to the weapon or method of murder used to commit the murder.

Of the Six remaining suspects, it will be found by careful examination of the available clues and testimony, that only four have a legitimate motive. The other two suspects may have been accused of having motives, but it will be found that those claims were either rumor, gossip, or lies.

Of the remaining four suspects, after careful examination of the clues and testimony, only two will be found to have a valid opportunity to commit the murder.

Of the remaining two suspects, after careful examination of clues and testimony, it will be found that one of them has a better alibi than the other, which leaves only one suspect without any legitimate alibi whatsoever, and therefore has the most reasonable opportunity to have committed the murder.

This formula is just one example. You could have it that 6 of 8 suspects have the opportunity, 4 of 6 have access to the weapon, and 2 of 4 have a legitimate motive, but one of these has a stronger motive than the other. Or even 6 of 8 have a legitimate motive, 4 of 6 have an opportunity, 2 of 4 have access to a weapon, but only one of them had access to the actual weapon used in the crime. Etcetera.

You do not have to follow any particular formula, but by the end of the scenario, the valid clues, legitimate evidence, and factual testimony should place the killer at the scene of the crime, at the time of death, with a motive, an opportunity, and access to the weapon, or the method used to commit the murder.

Here is the list of clues and who I decided to match them to. Do the same thing with your clues, and remember that the valid clues must match either the villain, the victim, or no one at all. The red herrings or false clues must not match the villain, they can match anyone else you like, but try not to match too many false clues to any single innocent suspect unless you absolutely have to.

> Teeth Marks (T) = Fortune Teller
>
> Ashes (T) = Fortune Teller
>
> Lipstick (T) = Fortune Teller
>
> Gunshot Residue(T) = no one / victim
>
> Revolver (T) = no one / victim
>
> Bullet Hole (T) = no one / establishes scene of the crime
>
> Pillow (T) = any one / establishes method / weapon
>
> Hair Sample (F) = Banker
>
> Lipstick Smudge #2 (F) = Beautician
>
> Dust (F) = Maid
>
> Bullet (T) = no one
>
> Hand Written Letter (F) = Constable

*The (T) or (F) notes which of the clues are valid (True), or a red herring (False).

Now that I have done that, I can easily cast doubt on the Banker, the Beautician, the Maid, and the Constable. They will appear to be linked directly to the crime somehow, and the players will try to find out how and why. But, what about the other suspects? The evidence, clues and red herrings only point to five out of eight suspects. We have three suspects unchecked as it were. There is a few things we can do to fix that, without physical evidence.

We can use witness testimony, lies, and gossip to give them access to one or more of the three essential factors involved in any murder mystery: Motive, Weapon (or method of murder), a possible Opportunity, or lack of a solid Alibi. We will give one, or two, of these incriminating factors to all of the innocent suspects. We will try not to give them all three, unless absolutely necessary. If we do, we must be sure that by the near conclusion of the game that there is some doubt for these innocent suspects. The villain absolutely must have access to the weapon, a motive and an opportunity.

In my example, it seems that most of the suspects have all three factors, however, three valid clues point directly at the Fortune Teller and this will help the sleuth's at the conclusion of the game, hopefully, identify her as the real culprit. To do that, they will have to determine which clues are valid and which are false. By carefully examining the evidence and by considering each suspects' testimony, they should be able to determine the truth. At least two of the valid clues will be found and place the killer at the scene of the crime when all is said and done.

All of this will be delivered through dialogue and actions during game play. Before we continue on to weapons, motives and opportunities, we need to place the clues into the story where they can be found by the players.

13. PLACING CLUES

As the players investigate the location of the body, they will need to find some of, or all of these clues. Later in the book I will give you ideas on how to make props for your clues, so you can place them at your crime scene. For right now, they are imaginary, but we have to decide where each clue is found, and how exactly it matches the possible suspects. Before deciding where you will place the clues in your scenario, consider where I decided to place the clues in my scenario as an example.

The first thing I need to place is the Teeth Marks clue. That is a little difficult to do, because it must, in this case, be on the victim or the villain. If the marks are on the victim, the players would need to find a way to match them to another suspects teeth. In this scenario, the only character who could successfully pull that off would be the Dentist. Everyone would want to know who bit the victim, and why. It could very well indicate that a struggle or a vicious fight took place between that suspect and the victim, either at the time of the murder, or some time previous to the victims demise. In this case, I decided the victim bit the villain while she was trying to smother him with the pillow -probably on her left arm.

This is pretty damning evidence straight away, but lets be clear that it would be nearly impossible for the suspects or sleuth's to figure out that the victim bit anyone. The villain would hide the mark on her arm, perhaps with the sleeves of her outfit, other wise it might get noticed. This is something she will definitely try to conceal any way that she can. This is a clue that I want to save for the solution and finale of the story, when someone will be able to suggest that the victim bit the villain, and someone has the bite marks on their body to prove it. The Dentist, at this point, would be able to completely redeem herself, if she can match the teeth of the victim to the marks on the villains' arm. Here is how it will eventually be done.

When the body is discovered, in the Billiards Room, there is a minute amount of blood in the corner of the victims mouth. It is not enough blood to take a sample from. Later, in Colby's Bedroom, a small amount of blood will also be found on the pillow, but not enough to take a sample from. This will at least suggest how the victim was killed, and establishes the cause of death. For awhile, the suspects will all have to assume the blood could just as likely be the victims as it could be the killers. The blood is, of course, the Fortune Tellers, but no one in this story will be able to prove that the blood matches, nor will they ever be allowed to inspect each-other for bite wounds, at least not until the very conclusion and solution to the game story.

The ashes will be found on the bed sheets in the victims bedroom, and the Tobacconist will eventually be able to match them to the brand of cigarettes that the Fortune Teller smokes. I might want to reason how the ashes were transferred from the villain to the crime scene. In this case, they are on the bed sheets, which would seem to suggest that she had a smoke in his room. If so, I have to add a cigarette butt to the list of clues, and perhaps an ashtray, unless she happened to toss the butt out his bedroom window. That could work, but the butt would now be outside on the ground where it could be found and examined. I decide, however, that does not fit this story, so perhaps she had a cigarette just prior to entering his room, that way the ashes are relevant but the cigarette butt is not. I will add that to the story line later, in the final details.

I should also make at least half of the suspects smokers so that each one could be a possible candidate for the ashes clue. There are a number of things I can do with the lipstick smudge. It could be on a cigarette butt in an ashtray, it could be on the bed sheets, the pillow, or perhaps on a cloth or paper napkin found crumpled up in a trash can.

The lipstick smudge will be found on the victims shirt collar. Why was the victim mostly clothed when found dead, if he had been sleeping at the time? Easy enough to explain, if we make sure to let everyone know that Colby Brenton drank too much, earlier that night. He probably just went to his room, flopped onto his bed, and passed out. I could have one of the suspects help him to his room and into bed. This would mean that one of the suspects was the last one to see Colby alive, making them a suspect of interest. Having Colby drunk and passed out, would also explain his lack of strength and focus later, when he was overpowered by the Fortune Teller as she smothered him to death with a pillow.

Now I know even more about the victim. Colby was a drinker, and a smoker, just to cast some doubt on the ashes present on his bed sheets. The Tobacconist, of course, would be able to figure out the ashes don't match the cigars he smokes. You will also remember, that Colby took a shot at the Fortune Teller when she attacked him. Why didn't anyone hear the gun shot, wake up, and discover the crime in progress? Easy enough to explain. It was a dark and stormy night at Brenton Manor. There was a rain and thunder storm all night long with bright peals of lighting and loud rumbling thunder, which covered the sound of the gunshot. The 'dark and stormy night' is a cliche of the genre, but I decide it must be.

I could even go so far as to say that Colby had a silencer on his revolver, if I change it to a pistol. Everyone would wonder why he owned a gun like that, and if he were a spy it would make perfect sense, but in this case, he is not. I know the gunshot residue, on Colby's hand, should be found by the Constable right away. That way the players will know there is something fishy about the location where the the body was found. When they do examine his body, they should be able to determine that he was not stabbed, shot, strangled or bludgeoned to death. His clothes are dry, so he was not drowned, this leaves two possible causes of death for them to determine. Either he was poisoned, or suffocated to death.

If there is no suspicion that his cause of death was even murder, he could have died of any number of natural causes. In this case, everyone knows Colby was in pretty good health, despite his drinking and smoking. Besides all that, this is a murder mystery game, the moderator of the game will let everyone know that Colby has been murdered by someone amongst them.

I have to wonder why the Fortune Teller bothered to move the body. She is not the strongest of characters in the story, and it must have been a laborious task for her. Perhaps she intended to hide the body, somewhere in the Billiard Room, until she could hide her tracks and cover up her crime. For the sake of the story, I will establish that the Billiard Room, is not too far from Colby's bedroom. Perhaps his room is just across the hall from the Billiards Room, or down the hall, a room or two away.

The revolver will be found on the floor next to his bed. The Constable, with his background in ballistics, would be the most likely character to discover the bullet hole in the ceiling. The weapon, being a pillow, would also be found in Colby's room, unless of course the Fortune Teller decided to move that also, but I can not think of any reason why she would. She was too busy trying to move a body, and knew a pillow could be linked to anyone with access to Colby's room. If the door was unlocked, it could be anyone.

The Fortune Teller could, if she had a copy of the key, or the actual key itself, lock the door to his room after moving the body. Perhaps she would later discard the key somewhere. Better yet, she planted it on one of the other suspects, this could become a wonderful plot device later in my story.

I could place the hair sample on the bed, but that might suggest some unusual activity was taking place between Colby and the Banker. It could be found on the floor, or on some other piece of furniture, or it could be on Colby's clothing when his body is found. If the hair is found in Colby's room, the players will want to know how it got there. Perhaps Colby and the Banker had a private argument in there, earlier that day. It would be suggestive that some kind of an altercation took place. If it is found on the victims clothes, it would also indicate there was some kind of recent contact between the two. In this case, I decide the hair is found on a chair in Colby's bedroom, so the Banker can sit on the hot seat for awhile during the course of the game.

Lipstick smudge #2 is found on the victims collar. Most of the suspects or sleuth's could not be positive if they are both from the same person or not, but the Beautician could easily determine this. Which is why I decided, lipstick smudge #2 must belong to her. She might want to lie and say they are both the same, because she does not want to be incriminated for the crime. Perhaps she has a darker secret to keep hidden. Perhaps she was one of Colby's lover girls. As a Beautician, there might not be much real scandal in this, if it is revealed, unless we give her a real good reason to want to keep it hidden. To figure out why, is simple enough, and here is how I will do it.

According to statistics, most murders are committed by someone close to the victim. The first person to come into question, is usually the victims spouse. I will find Colby a wife for the story and make her one of the suspects. She can not be the Maid, because the Maid is an employee of the Manor. It could be the Beautician, but she could easily explain away her lipstick on the collar, because she would be the victims wife. It could be the Fortune Teller, but we have already established that this is a red herring, and it must not be hers. That leaves the Dentist. Perfect.

So, if the Beautician is desperate to hide her affair from everyone, we can easily reason this if she is related to the Dentist. The Beautician becomes the Dentists' sister. Interesting. There is some shady back story and subplot developing now. I am now learning even more about the suspects and their relation to the victim and to each other.

The Dust will also be found on the victims clothing. It will also be discovered on the Maids uniform. Sadly, she is the only one who can establish a match between dust samples. Even so, the players that discover the dust will see that it is somehow linked to the Maid, even if they can not prove it. Of course she will shrug it off, with the following statement, 'So what about the dust? I'm the Maid, I clean and dust here all day. There are any number of ways I could have gotten this dust on me. The dust you see on Colby's clothing matches the dust found in his room. I do clean his room occasionally as well, as you might imagine, it is my job after-all.'

What if at this exact moment, someone notices the key to Colby's bedroom in her pocket, or it falls out of her pocket? Remember that, at some point, the Fortune Teller could have planted it on her. She might be shocked at first, a normal reaction, but she could go on to say, 'I do have access to all the keys of the Mansion, do I need remind you that I work here?' Her statement is valid, but leaves her a little suspicious nonetheless. I shall therefore, add a key to the list of clues.

The bullet will be found in the room to serve as a minor distraction, and the possibility for some impromptu role-playing on the part of the players. The handwritten letter must be found also. It could be in the room, or even better, I will have it folded up in the victims back pocket, but sticking out just enough for someone to notice it after awhile. The Constable can not be the one to find it, because if he does, he will try to conceal it.

Reason being, is that whatever it says may incriminate him, if the Banker can match their handwriting styles, or if the Fortune Teller can match a fingerprint on it, to that of the Constables hand. If it's a friendly letter, the Constable would not care, but then it would not be a red herring either. I will decide it's a threat. Why is the Constable threatening Colby, and what kind of threat is it? If Colby had done something wrong, the Constable might just easily press charges, and arrest him. It must be a little more personal than that.

Here is what I will do to answer a few questions in the story that need answering. The letter does point suspicion on the Constable, because it is a threat note, but what if the nature of the note reveals a prime element of the plot, and a possible motive for the Fortune Teller? The note, at this point, becomes a red herring with a hidden factual clue in it. The Letter, I decide, reads as follows:

Mr. Colby Brenton, if you do not end your affair with my wife very soon you will deeply regret it! You had better break it off with her as soon as possible, or I will be forced to deal with the situation however I see fit! I can and will ruin you, if you do not comply! You know who this is, and you know that I mean business. You know that I have the means to carry out my words.

Now the letter seems to implicate the Constable, or perhaps the Banker. How? They are the only two male suspects that are married. It is true that the Bankers' wife is not a suspect, nor is she even present, but that does not matter. The Banker could still have written the note, and if he did, he probably would not want to match the handwriting styles, because he would implicate himself in the crime by doing so. When he is cooperative in matching handwriting samples, everyone will know he could not be the author of the letter. This leaves the Constable. Either way, the players will never know if the letter is a valid clue or a red herring anyways.

By this time, however, it should have already been revealed that the Constables' wife is, of course, the Fortune Teller. She is probably familiar with his hand writing, and may or may not, reveal this information. If she does so, she must either confess to or deny having an affair with Colby.

Either way, everyone will now suspect that they were having illicit relations. She might even wish to ask her husband why he never confronted her about it. It gives the Constable a motive for killing Colby, but cleverly hidden is also the Fortune Tellers motive. I will tell you what that is in the next section. First, lets be sure to note all of the clues and their location in the scenario, for future reference.

Teeth Marks: On Madame Edwinas' left arm.

Ashes: On Colby's Bed.

Lipstick Smudge#1: On the victims collar.

Gunshot Residue: On the victims right hand and wrist.

Revolver: On the floor near the bed in Colby's bed room.

Bullet Hole: In the ceiling above the bed in Colby's room.

Pillow: On Colby's Bed.

Hair Sample: On the chair in Colby's bed room.

Lipstick Smudge#2: On the victims collar.

Dust: On the victims clothing and on the Maids outfit and in Colby's room.

Bullet: On the Night stand in Colby's bed room.

Hand Written Threat Letter: Folded up in the victims back pocket, sticking out a bit.

Key to Colby's Bedroom Door: In the Maids pocket.

Broken Pocket Watch reading 12:45: In Colby's pocket.

Note: You can use clues to establish information such as time of death, or scene of the crime, not every clue has to point to a suspect. A clue could even suggest a weapon, motive, or some ones opportunity to commit the crime, or determine some ones alibi to be false. Be creative with the clues that you will use in your story. For example, I could add one more clue to establish time of death.

During the struggle, the victim or the villain could have knocked over an alarm clock, on the night stand near the bed. When it fell to the floor it broke. When the players find this clock on the floor it could still read the time, as it were, when it was broken. Instead of using that idea and writing it into the story, I decided to add a slightly different clue to the list that will help establish the time of Colby Brenton's death. Someone will find a broken pocket watch, which will read 12:45, in Colby's pocket, and I added it to the list of clues.

13a. Who finds each Clue?

For future reference, while writing out the scenario, we should decide who will find each clue, if we have not done so already, and make a list of it. The person who finds a clue does not have to be an expert or have any skill in evaluating the clue, and in most cases, we would want suspects to find clues they do not have the ability to understand, so that they will be forced to interact with the others in order to make sense of a particular clue. Be sure to have your villain find at least one clue, or everyone will be suspicious of the one person who did not find a clue. If possible, try to make sure that all suspects find at least one clue. Here are the notes:

Teeth Marks: (if found) Lisa Brenton, the Dentist.

Ashes: Found by Lance Gibbins, the Banker.

Gunshot Residue: Found by Derryl Gramlich, the Constable.

Lipstick Smudge #1: Found by Claire Ruppel.

Revolver: Found by Derryl Gramlich.

Pillow: Found by Lisa Brenton, Dentist.

Hair: Found by Erik Macha, the Barber.

Lipstick Smudge#2: Found by Claire Ruppel.

Dust: Found by Benita Lintner, the Maid.

Bullet: Found by Benita Lintner, the Maid.

Handwritten Letter: Found by Nelson Brenton, the Tobacconist.

Broken Pocket Watch: Found by Madame Edwina, the Fortune Teller.

Key to Colby's Bedroom: Found by Lisa Brenton, the Dentist.

14. WEAPONS, MOTIVES, AND OPPORTUNITIES

We know who the murderer is now, and how she committed the crime. In this particular story, the weapon was a pillow that pretty much anyone could have had access to, provided they also had an opportunity to commit the crime. In the 'Cause of Death Chart', I gave some examples for different types of weapons that could be used, depending on the victims cause of death. A vast variety of interesting and mundane weapons could be used in your scenarios, so long as the weapon you choose is consistent with your victims cause of death.

Use your imagination, and choose a weapon that fits the method of the crime. Be sure that, if the weapon should become a clue, that it can somehow be linked to the killer and to some of the other suspects as well. They do not all need to be the owner of the weapon in question, but if they are to be linked to it, they must have at least had access to the weapon or method used to kill the victim.

For example, in the case of a murder mystery where it is determined that the victim was killed by blunt force trauma, you could have some of your suspects have access to a weapon that is capable of being used and consistent with the cause of death or the method of murder. All but one of those weapons would be red herrings. The sleuth's or suspects would need to find a way to determine and prove which weapon was actually used. Then they would need to determine which suspects had access to the actual weapon, and try to find a way to link it to the true villain. This example would make a great story device for any murder mystery scenario.

We will make sure the killer in the mystery has an opportunity and no solid alibi. All of the suspects can have, or claim to have, an alibi, but they must be shaky at best. Be sure to give the best opportunities to the primary suspects and assign them the weakest possible alibis. An example of the best alibi ever would be that a suspect was in jail during the time of the crime. That is an example of a really solid alibi. A suspect with that type of alibi, however, would not be a suspect at all.

An example of a poor alibi, and a possible opportunity, would be if the suspect claimed to be in the bathroom during the time of the crime. It is unlikely there are any witnesses to vouch for them. Their alibi may very well be true but without proof it is quite questionable. All of your suspects should have at least a slight chance of being able to commit the murder, some should have better opportunities than others obviously. Those with secrets to hide will try to establish the best alibis, even if they are lies.

Suspects Alibis or Opportunities to commit the murder may depend on where they were within proximity to the general location of the crime scene at the exact or general time the murder was committed. Be sure to make a list of the suspects and note their opportunity or alibi, or both.

As I discussed before, all the suspects should appear to have a motive. They will either have a legitimate motive, an implication of a motive, or an accusation of a motive, which may or may not be entirely true. The innocent suspects, including the liar, should definitely have two out of three, when it comes to a weapon, motive or an opportunity. So, they should either have access to the weapon (or the means), and a legitimate motive, or they should have access to the weapon and an opportunity, or they should have a legitimate motive and a legitimate opportunity. Like this:

Innocent Suspects (Including the Liar)

Weapon & Motive = Yes, Opportunity = No, Alibi = True
Or...
Weapon & Opportunity = Yes, Motive = No, Alibi = False
Or...
Motive & Opportunity = Yes, Weapon = No, Alibi = False

Villain Suspect

Weapon & Motive & Opportunity = Yes, Alibi = False

The villain will, of course, have a rather difficult time producing a believable alibi, but rest assured they should try. In this case, the Fortune Teller will claim she was in bed asleep, which is shaky, but fair enough considering everyone else's alibi would be pretty much the same.

We could have the Constable vouch for her, saying they were sleeping in the same room all night, and as far as he knows she was there the whole night. If he is a real deep sleeper, he would never have noticed her getting out of bed to visit Colby in his bedroom, especially if the sound of thunder might cover her footsteps across the old creaky wooden floor. Then again, if the storm was so loud, perhaps everyone had a fairly restless night trying to sleep through the storm. I will decide he takes medication, which helps him sleep, and she was able to use this fact to her advantage.

The question now becomes: Why did she do it? Your villain should have a solid motive to commit such a heinous crime. There are many motives for someone to commit a murder and you can do the research from true crime stories to come up with a number of possible motives, but here is the list I use, which encompasses the classic motives used in many murder mysteries.

Chart#9 MOTIVES FOR SUSPECTS AND KILLERS

Roll D20
1. Hatred / Scorn: The villain hated the victim. A hate crime is an example.
2. Jealousy: The villain was jealous of the victim or someone else.
3. Fear: The villain was afraid of the victim. Could be self defense.
4. Betrayal: The victim somehow betrayed the villain. Broken trust.
5. Money / Greed: This could be an inheritance. Money from insurance policies.
6. Opposition: The villain and victim were competitors for some common objective.
7. Lust: The villain wanted the victim all to themselves.
8. Revenge / Retaliation: The victim had done something nasty to the villain in the past.
9. Insanity: The villain is either insane or temporarily insane. Perhaps has mental issues.
10. The victim knew too much too live: The villain ends their life to cover up a dark secret.
11. Black Mail: The victim was blackmailing the villain and they got tired of it.
12. Contract Killing: The villain has been hired or paid to kill the victim.
13. Rivalry: The villain and victim were long time rivals or enemies.
14. Envy: The villain wanted something that the victim had for themselves.
15. Obsession: The villain loved the victim but it was unrequited.
16. Protection: The villain killed the victim to protect someone else from some kind of harm.
17. Conviction: The villain killed the victim to settle a matter they thought was morally wrong.
18. Passion: The villain and victim were competitors for the same lover.
19. Ambition: The villain would gain professional power, promotion or political advancement.
20. Mercy: The mercy killing is done out of compassion to end perceived suffering.

Using Chart#9, I rolled a D20, and came up with a 7, which would indicate my Fortune Tellers' motive for murdering Colby was somehow related to Lust. I find the exact motive is hidden and revealed in the Constables threat letter to Colby. Sadly, Colby will never get to tell anyone what exactly happened that night. Colby had read the note and he did not want any trouble with the Constable. He knew the Constable was serious. He intended to end his affair with the Fortune Teller, and he did.

The Fortune Teller did sneak into his room that night, but not with intentions of murder. She was hoping to get a little bit of attention from her secret lover. She was not aware her husband knew about the affair. He never confronted her about it because he really loved her, and was hoping to work things out with her. So, the Fortune Teller goes and sneaks into Colby's room. Wakes him up for some attention. He is still drunk, but just coherent enough to tell her she should go back to bed and be with her husband. He tells her the affair is over and he does not want to see her ever again. She becomes enraged, kills him with the pillow. We already know what transpired after this, but now the motive is clear, but it is not just lust or anger, the motive in this case becomes a broken heart. The Fortune Teller was in love with Colby, or at least she truly believed she was.

Now we have to wonder why Colby and his wife, the Dentist, were not sleeping in the same room. Easily explained. They are currently separated but trying to work things out. She is completely oblivious to his affairs but very aware of his serious drinking and money problems. She might have a clue about his affairs, but perhaps she is in serious denial. What will she do when she finds out her sister and husband were having relations? What will she do if she finds out about the Fortune Teller, and a rumor that Colby was also having relations with the Maid? I don't know for certain either, but I can venture a fair guess. Perhaps we will find out when the scenario finally plays out.

So far we have established the motive for the Fortune Teller and a possible motive for the Constable, which would be Jealousy, or perhaps Rage. We will give every suspect a motive which may or may not be true.

As Colby's wife, the Dentist would stand to gain some monetary benefit, if Colby died before she did. He did have an excellent insurance policy. Her motive becomes Money. The Tobacconist would not seem to have anything to gain from Colby's death, unless we make him Colby's younger brother. He could likely become heir to the Estate and Manor. His motive becomes Greed. We will say the Barber disliked the victim, and his motive becomes Hatred or Disdain.

I decide the Beautician, the Dentists sister, does not have any known motive, but her actions in the game will cast enough doubt on her, and everyone will be trying to figure out what she is trying to hide. If she has any motive at all, it might be Humiliation, but her motive involves covering up her affair with Colby. She probably wanted to end the affair, which she intended to do, but one thing led to another, and they were making out in his room before he passed out for the night.

Colby's wife, the Dentist, had been the first one to go to bed that night, claiming she had a serious migraine, and was going to take some heavy duty pain medication. She would be unaware of her sisters actions from that point on. In the morning, the Dentist may also show everyone her pills hoping that it makes for a good alibi, but there is no way she can really prove that she even took them.

The Maid will not have any real motive either, but someone will claim she was being Blackmailed to work for Colby for free, and someone will accuse her of having relations with him. None of it will be true, but she will admit that Colby was somewhat of a womanizer and she felt she was a victim of sexual harassment. It sounds like a possible motive, but not a very strong one. Most everyone would ask why she has not quit, the answer is clear, Colby pays her well to do her job, she is very pretty, and perhaps he even bribes her to keep quiet about his lecherous activities. She needs the money, and she complies willingly. So, if anyone was being blackmailed it was Colby, not the Maid.

The Banker is an associate of the family and has been for a long time. Colby borrowed a lot of money from the Banker to pay off gambling debts and never payed him back. Colby might be getting by on the family money, but he has nearly squandered away the majority of it. The Bankers motive might become Money.

All of my suspects might have access to the weapon, an opportunity, and a possible motive. We do not always want it to work out this way, but for this particular story it had to be. The players trying to solve this mystery will have to rely on careful examination of the clues and witness testimony to solve the case.

There is still, however, a lot more work we have to do. We have to figure out who will know what about the others, what they will reveal about themselves, and what they will try to conceal. Eventually, we will also want to create a time line to chart the events that transpired throughout the night, up until the point that someone finds the body in the Billiards Room. For now, lets make a list of the suspects, and note their possible motives for future reference. Here is an example based on the Murder at Brenton Manor scenario.

Lisa Brenton (Dentist) Money -From an insurance policy.

Derryl Gramlich (Constable) Jealousy or Rage -Colby was sleeping with his wife.

Claire Ruppel (Beautician) Humiliation / False -She had no reason to want Colby dead.

Erik Macha (Barber) Disdain / Hatred -Did not like Colby`s Political Affiliations.

Lance Gibbins (Banker) Money -Colby owed him a lot of money.

Benita Lintner (Maid) Blackmail / Sexual Harassment / -False

Madame Edwina (Fortune Teller) Lust / Rage / Broken Heart -Colby broke up with her.

Nelson Brenton (Tobacconist) Greed -He could be heir to the Manor and the Estate.

Note that I needed a reason for the Barber, Erik Macha, to dislike Colby. I decided it has something to do with Politics, because it is one of many reasons people might decide they do not like someone or cant get along with them. Politics and Religion are the subjects that most people argue about in real life. If you really need specifics, on the following page, there are two simple charts to establish political and religious beliefs. Religion and Politics may not have any real place in your story, or it may very well become a crucial aspect of the plot. It is up to you.

14a Politics and Religion

Chart#10 Politics

(D10)

1) Anarchist
2) Communist
3) Democrat
4) Republican
5) Constitutionalist
6) Libertarian
7) Socialist
8) Fascist
9) Capitalist
10) Secret Society (see chart #12)

Chart#11 Religion

(D10)

1) Atheist
2) Agnostic
3) Theist
4) Paganism
5) Taoism
6) Confucianism
7) Gnostic
8) Metaphysical
9) Polytheist
10) Occultism

Chart#12 Secret Society

(D10)

1) Bilderberg Group
2) Bohemian Club
3) Freemason
4) Rosicrutian Order
5) Illuminati
6) Knights Templar
7) Majesty Twelve
8) Scientology
9) Skull and Bones
10) Thule Society

15. CREATING SUSPECTS

The next thing we will work on is the Suspect Sheets, which will contain all of the information each suspect will know about themselves, and what they know, or think they know, about the others. It may also include what they know, or think they know, about the victim. It should also contain what information (true or false) they might gather from the crime scene itself, and possible suggestions on how the character could evaluate the evidence and clues found as the game progresses. For the most part, the Suspect Sheets are for your reference only.

You will use the data for writing the story and the time line, and it will also let you know what information should be revealed to the players as it is relevant during the game. Some of the 'safe' information you will probably give to your players at the time you invite them to your party. Some information will be given to them ahead of time, as they will need to know general information about the role they will play, how to dress, what props to bring, and how to act when they show up for the party.

I will discuss later in this guide what information should be revealed during each stage of your entire murder mystery party, so that everything will run as smoothly as possible. We will also create the 'safe' player versions of these sheets as well, which will be called 'Character Dossiers'. Before we get started, we should consult the scenario notes and updated victim notes as they are so far.

Case: Murder at Brenton Manor
Theme: The Roaring 1920's (1922)
Location: Brenton Manor, Manitou Springs -Colorado
Event: Colby Brenton's Celebration Party, He got a big gig at a popular local venue.

Victim: Colby Brenton, Male, 34yrs old
Occupation: Amateur Jazz Musician, plays Sax at a few local venues.
Marital Status: Married to Lisa Brenton -Dentist

Family: Younger brother is Nelson Brenton -Tobacconist

In-laws: Sister in law is Claire Ruppel -Beautician and sister of Lisa Brenton -Dentist

Employees: Benita Lintner -Maid

Friends: none of note

Finances: Comfortable monetary income, but in debt to Lance Gibbins -Banker

Secrets: Several affairs

Habits: Heavy drinker and smoker of cigars.

Political Affiliations: Republican

Religion: Theist

Acquaintances: (below)

Constable Derryl Gramlich

Erik Macha -Barber

Lance Gibbins -Banker

Madame Edwina -Psychic Consultant and Fortune Teller

Cause of Death: Suffocation / Smothering -death by pillow

Time of Death: 12:45 AM on 8/11/1922

Place of Body: Found in the Billiards Room

Scene of Crime: His Bedroom

Villain: Madame Edwina

Liar: Claire Ruppel

Who Found the Body: The Butler (game host)

Suspects List: (below)

Fortune Teller -Madame Edwina

Beautician -Claire Ruppel

Dentist -Lisa Brenton

Barber -Erik Macha

Banker -Lance Gibbons

Maid -Benita Lintner

Tobacconist -Nelson Brenton

Constable -Derryl Gramlich

Note that I needed to establish who found the body. In some cases, the person that finds the body immediately becomes a suspect, and will be questioned as such. It can be one of your suspects, or it can be a third party, who could not have been involved. As the real host and moderator of the game, you can choose to play the part of a truly innocent guest, who will be a narrator and referee during the game. You will be guiding or directing the suspects and sleuth's as needed so that the story can progress through the scenario in a logical way.

In most murder mystery games, the moderator will sometimes play a Detective, so as to keep the game running it's course, but I see no reason for this to be absolutely necessary. I think we can all remember how much fun the Butler had, in that comedy mystery movie, based on the famous table top board game of the same name.

You could also, perhaps, decide to play the part of Colby Brenton during the dinner celebration party. You would act out his characters actions and dialogue for that part of the story. It is up to you how you wish to play all of that out. I decide that when I host this game that I will play the part of Colby Brenton through dinner. In the 'morning' stage of the game, I will not only be the moderator and referee, but I will also play the part of the truly innocent Butler, who discovered the body, and who guides the rest of the story as necessary.

This time the Butler did not do it. Lets start making 'Character Sheets' for the suspects.
On the following page is the format I use to establish all the information I will need for my own reference, and for writing the player character Dossiers later.

Name: (gender)   Age:

Marital Status:

Occupation:

Areas of Expertise:

Political Affiliation:

Religion:

Relation to the Victim:

Relations to Other Suspects:

Hobbies:

Habits:

Guilt Status:

Weapon:

Motive:

Opportunity:

Alibi:

Clues to Reveal:

Clues to Conceal:

How you did it:

What you know about the others:

#1:

#2:

#3:

#4:

During Examination of the Body:

During Questioning:

Here is a step by step method using the format described on the previous.

Step#1   Determine the Gender for the character.

Step#2   Name the character as described in Chapter 6a.

Step#3   Determine the Age for the character as described in Chapter 6b.

Step#4   Determine characters Marital Status. (Single, In a Relationship, Married, Divorced)

Step#4   Note the Occupation of the character you selected.

Step#5   Note the Area of Expertise of the character as it relates to their occupation.

Step#6   Assign a Political Affiliation if needed. See Chart#10.

Step#7   Assign a Religion if needed. See Chart#11

Step#8   Establish how this character is related to the victim. You might wish to write this information after the story is clear and all of the character sheets are completed. You can use Chart #14 if needed.

Step#10 Decide what Hobbies this character may be interested in. (See Chart#16 for examples)

Step#11 Decide what Habits this character may have. (See Chart#16 for examples)

Step#12 Note the Guilt Status of the character. (Villain or Liar or Innocent)

Step#13 Note if this character owns, or has access to the weapon or method of murder. You may want half of your suspects to have access to a weapon or method of the murder.

Step#14 Establish a motive for the character as described in Chapter 14 and Chart#9. All suspects should either have or appear to have a motive for committing the murder.

Step#15 Note if and how this character had an opportunity to commit the crime. You may want the other half of your suspects who do not have access to a weapon to have an opportunity.

Step#16 Describe the Alibi this character has or claims to have. All suspects will try to have an alibi, but perhaps one or two may confess that they do not.

Step#17 Determine which informational clues this character will have to reveal. You might wish to write this information only after the story is clear and all the character sheets are completed.

Step#18 Determine which informational clues this character will want to hide. You might wish to write this information after the story is clear and all of the character sheets are completed.

Step#19 How you did it: This is only described for the villain, and will be used to write a confession. You do not need to note this on the innocent suspect sheets.

Step #20 Establish what four pieces of information this character knows, or thinks they know, about the others. You might wish to write this information after the story is clear and all of the character sheets are completed. I will describe how to determine who knows what about who in Chapter 16.

Step#21 Describe how the character will act during investigation of the body, and what clues they might find. You might wish to write this information after the story is clear and all of the character sheets are completed. Use your clue notes and story notes as reference.

Step#22 Describe how the character will act and react during questioning. You might wish to write this information after the story is clear and all of the character sheets are completed.

15a. The Villain

Lets make the villains Suspect Sheet first. Here is what the villains Suspect Sheet will look like in the Murder at Brenton Manor example.

<u>MADAME EDWINA</u>

Name: Madame Edwina   (female)   Age: 42

Marital Status: Married

Occupation: Psychic Consultant and Fortune Teller

Areas of Expertise: Matching fingerprint / handprint samples.

Political Affiliation: Un-affiliated

Religion: Metaphysical Spirituality

Hobbies: Astrology, Studying the Occult.

Habits: Smoker. You do not drink.

Relation to the Victim: You were an acquaintance of Colby Brenton, he was fascinated with Astrology and Tarot and he often consulted with you for advice concerning love and money.

Relations to Other Suspects: You are married to the Constable, Derryl Gramlich. The two of you have an unusual marriage. Derryl works a lot and you run a small Psychic Consultation business.

Guilt Status: You are the Villain!

Weapon: A Pillow. You had access to the weapon or method of murder.

Motive: Heart Break. Colby Brenton broke off your affair the night of the murder.

Opportunity: Derryl was on medication to help him sleep. You could have easily snuck out of bed and into Colby's room to kill him.

Alibi: You claim to have been asleep in a guest bedroom with your husband. You may also claim to be very weak and tired and in poor health these days.

Clues to Reveal: You are a smoker. (Opportunity) You will admit your husband is a heavy sleeper and a snorer not to mention a bed hog. (Relation) You must admit to having known the victim, that you were his psychic consultant.

Clues to Conceal: (Motive) You claim to have no motive for killing Colby Brenton but you really did. Colby broke off his affair with you. You must try to conceal your affair with Colby Brenton because you do not want to be incriminated, and you do not want your husband to find out. If the lipstick smudges are revealed, you will try to hide that one of them is yours. Do not reveal what you know about Benita, the Maid, and Lance, the Banker, until the right moment. When you were smoking on the Balcony you saw a shadowy figure walking around in the garden, possibly a man. You can not reveal this until someone suggests you went to the Balcony for a smoke or you will be caught in a lie.

What you know about the others:

#1: (T) Lisa Brenton (Dentist) had recently taken out an insurance policy on her husband, Colby Brenton. She would have gotten a lot of money if Colby were to die an untimely death.

#2: (T) Colby Brenton was in some financial troubles and owed Lance Gibbins a lot of money.

#3: (F) Benita Lintner (the Maid) was being blackmailed, by Colby Brenton, to work at the Manor for free, but you are not sure what dark secrets he was blackmailing her with.

#4: (F) You claim that Colby Brenton told you several times that he was afraid that his wife wanted to have him killed.

How you did it: You woke up early in the morning, around 12:15 AM, from a bad dream. You needed a cigarette, so you left the guest bed room and went down the hall, and out on to the balcony to smoke. Your husband Derryl is allergic to your smoke, and you thought the smell might wake him up. While you were out there smoking, you got to thinking about your love affair with Colby. You finished smoking and discarded the cigarette butt over the side of the balcony. You decided to sneak into his room for some attention. The door was unlocked, you went in and closed the door behind you. When you arrived, at 12:30 AM, Colby was asleep. You may have noticed a lip stick smudge on his collar, but realize it could have been his wife's, so you did not give it much thought. You crawled on to the bed, straddled Colby, and woke him up by kissing him on his neck. When he awoke, he seemed groggy and still drunk. He got a little angry that you disturbed his sleep and told you that he needed to talk to you. He told you the affair was over and that you should go back to your room to be with your husband. At about 12:40 AM you asked him if he loved you, and he said no. You were heartbroken and became enraged. In a moment of angry passion, you decided that if you could not have Colby, no one else would either. You placed your hands over Colby's throat hoping to choke him, but you were not strong enough. He struggled and bit your left arm. Colby was still very drunk and was not able to put up much of a fight. You grabbed a pillow and placed it over his face to suffocate him, using all of your body weight, he was not able to resist. He grabbed the revolver from the night stand by the bed and took a shot at you. At that precise moment, loud thunder covered the sound of the gun fire, and Colby died at 12:45 AM. The revolver fell to the floor. You killed him. A moment later you came to your senses and realized what you had just done. You took a key from the night stand that you recognized would lock Colby's bedroom door. You put the key in your pocket. In a state of panic, you decided to try and hide Colby's body somewhere it would not be discovered for quite some time. After opening the bedroom door and looking down the hall to see if the coast was clear, you dragged Colby out of bed, out of his room and down the hall to the Billiards Room. You were hoping to hide him in the closet of this room, but it was locked. You were physically exhausted by then and gave up the idea of moving Colby's body any further. Besides that, you were aware that the Maid was prowling around the house and that some of the other guests might be awake as well. On your way back to the guest room, you closed and locked Colby's door. You decided you would plant the key on another guest sometime later. In the morning, you planted it in the Maids pocket.

During Examination of the Body: You act horrified. You will notice Dust on the victims clothing, you will also notice it on the Maids outfit. You will bring it to the attention of the other suspects. Perhaps you pretend to be disgusted by the sight of the corpse. Perhaps act faintish as if you are going to pass out. Maybe sit down somewhere and fan yourself. You could say you need fresh air and/or a glass of water.

During Questioning: If given a chance to read the threat note, found in the victims pocket, you can match a fingerprint on it to the fingerprint of your husbands hand, or you can just simply suggest the handwriting is familiar to you as that of your husbands. However, you must realize at this point that you must deny the affair. If your husband tells you he knew about the affair you will be forced to confess the truth, but state you hid this secret because you did not want your husband to find out. Once you have confessed to the affair, you should shrug it off as if it is not so important as asking your husband to explain why he never confronted you about it, and furthermore, why he was threatening Colby. You do not have any real love for your husband, so in reality you do not mind passing the shadow of suspicion upon him now as your strategy to cover up your crime. Once it is established you were having the affair with Colby, you should claim that you were deeply in love with him and had no reason to want him dead. Try to reveal what you know about Lisa if she starts asking too many questions about you. If it is ever revealed you went to the Balcony for a smoke, shrug it off and just explain you forgot to mention it as it did not seem important to you. Point out the dust on the body and on the Maids outfit.

How to cover your crime: You might suggest at some point that the Maid would have access to the keys to the Manor and that she could have an opportunity to kill Colby. You know she has a key on her because you planted it there, but you can not admit to it directly. Once everyone knows about your affair, use what assets you have to cast suspicion on your husband. Also try to share what you know about the others. If it is pointed out that one of the lipstick smudges might match your brand of lipstick, you will recall the other was on his collar when you went to visit Colby in his bed room. You will suggest the Beautician, Claire Ruppel, could shed some light on the matter. Here is what you could say:

"How interesting, I would not have any idea on how that could have gotten there, how can we even be sure who those belong to? Perhaps they are from Lisa. They are married after-all. They could suggest any woman present. Why don't we ask Claire, the Beautician to sort this out, I am sure she has some experience in cosmetics."

If someone suggests the ashes might match your particular brand of cigarettes, you could say:

"Everyone knows that Colby smoked cigars. I am not the only one who smokes around here as you might have noticed. Those ashes could have come from the hearth for all we know."

If someone asks you if you saw your husband take his sleeping pills, you will say yes.

Alright, that is almost everything we need to know about the villain. Note that I added a (T) for True, and a (F) for False, next to each piece of information she knows about the others. In every scenario you create with this system, your villain will always share at least two true and at least two false pieces of information with the others. Reason being is to make their role more challenging. The villain will not, of course, reveal which are true or false and will not even really know one way or the other.

You only need to note whether each statement is true or false on your version of the character sheets. Note that Madame Edwina's character sheet clearly reveals that she is the killer and how she did it and how to cover her tracks. What if we do not want this player to know if they are guilty or not during the game? This version of her sheet is for your reference only. In a later chapter I will show you how to create Character Dossiers for your players. The 'safe' version of all the players character sheets will not tell them their guilt status, weapon, motive, opportunity or any information or hints that would give this information away to them.

When I write a murder mystery game scenario, I find it is more fun, and more spontaneous for the players to act out their characters if no one knows their guilt status in the game. At the end of the game, and the votes have been counted, it is a lot of fun to see the suspects all sitting around in anticipation wondering who the real villain is.

15b. The Liar

Now we need to make character sheets for the remaining suspects, who are all innocent, except one will be the liar in the game. The liar and the villain will never be the same suspect. Lets create the liar next.

What I need to do now is determine which of the suspects should be the liar. Using logic and reason, I decide the Beautician, Claire Ruppel, will make the perfect candidate, and here is why. So far, we already know she has a big secret to hide, and if she is too cooperative matching lipstick smudge samples, she will not only incriminate herself, but she will also reveal the other matches the villain. I want her to inadvertently cover the trail of the Fortune Teller, although she is not consciously trying to accomplish this. She wants to avoid matching the lipstick samples because she already knows for a fact that one is probably her own.

CLAIRE RUPPEL

Name: Claire Ruppel   (female)   Age: 29

Marital Status: Single

Occupation: Beautician / Hair Stylist

Area of Expertise: You can match lip stick samples to cosmetic brands and match hair samples.

Political Affiliation: Democrat

Religion: Theist

Hobbies: You like to dance.

Habits: Chew bubble gum. Smoker. Casual drinker.

Relation to the Victim: You are Colby Brenton's sister-in-law.

Relations to Other Suspects: You are Lisa Brenton's sister.

Guilt Status: You are the Liar! But, you are innocent of murder.

Weapon: None. It will be determined that you could have had access to the weapon.

Motive: Humiliation and a Dark Secret. (You were having an affair with Colby Brenton)

Opportunity: It will be revealed that you could have had an opportunity and a weak alibi.

Alibi: You claim to have been in your room the entire night.

Clues to Reveal: You should reveal your relation to the victim and to his wife, your sister. You must reveal that you smoke and drink.

Clues to Conceal: You were having an affair with Colby. You do not want your sister to find out. You will want to avoid matching the lip stick smudge samples, because you know one of them is yours, and it will reveal your dark secret. You do not want to pin them wrongfully on anyone else either. You do not know who killed Colby. You were the last person to see Colby alive, before he was murdered. After your sister went to bed, you went to visit Colby in his bedroom at around 11:45 PM. You intended to break off the affair, but he was charming with his words and actions. One thing led to another, and the two of you made out for awhile. You accidentally left a lip stick smudge on his collar. Colby was still drunk when you went to see him, and after the brief make out session, he passed out and fell asleep.

What you know about the others:

#1: (T) Nelson Brenton (the Tobacconist) has a motive: He is Colby Brenton's younger brother and would become a likely Heir to the Estate and the Manor.

#2: (F) You claim you overheard a vicious argument between Erik Macha (the Barber) and Colby Brenton (the victim) the day before around 4:45 PM, taking place in Colby Brenton's room. The door was closed, so you can not be positive about what was said, but it sounded like a very heated discussion involving money and embezzlement. This event took place before Dinner was served that night. You were walking by Colby's room, after using the bath room to freshen up, and you were on your way downstairs to the Lounge. You saw Erik Macha leaving Colby's room later, around 5:00 PM.

#3: (F) The Lipstick Smudges probably match Lisa Brenton's particular brand of cosmetics. (Remember that she is Colby's wife, and your sister.)

#4: (F) You suggest that Benita Lintner, the Maid, was having an affair with Colby Brenton, and that he was paying her for 'certain' favors. You will also suggest the lipstick smudges might match her brand of cosmetics.

During Examination of the Body: You will notice the lipstick smudges, but say nothing about them because you already know one of them is yours, and it might incriminate you and reveal your dark secret. You will notice some Dust on the victims clothing and point it out. You will notice there are no physical bruises or markings on the body and suggest that Colby may have been poisoned.

During Questioning: You will try to reveal what you know, or think you know, about the other suspects and what you might know about the victim. You will claim to have no real motive to commit the crime. At some point, you may have an opportunity to match a hair sample found during the investigation. It will match Lance Gibbins (the Bankers) hair color and length. You may be asked to match the lip stick smudge samples to cosmetics, but you are trying to avoid doing this. If forced to do so, one smudge is yours, the other is Edwina's. You have always disliked Colby's Maid. You claim you have suspected her of stealing from the Manor several times and suggested it to Colby, but he ignored your accusations. You may also be asked if it is true that your sister, Lisa Brenton, was ever accused of killing her ex-husband. This has been a big hush-hush dirty secret in the family for a long time. The truth is yes. Her ex-husband was murdered. He was suffocated to death with a pillow. Lisa Brenton was the prime suspect. Her ex-husband was extremely abusive. She was tried in court but there was a mistrial on lack of evidence. She was acquitted of the charges and the case was dropped.

Alright, we have covered everything the Beautician will need to know on how to play her character. Notice that she likes to chew bubble gum. Chewing Gum could make a great clue in your murder mystery, if you can put it somewhere at the crime scene, and link it to one or more suspects. In this case, it is nothing more than a prop.

You could also use the liar as an accomplice in your murder mystery scenarios, covering or vouching for the villain, and perhaps may even have assisted in the general act of the crime itself, but remember that the villain must have to be the one who actually performed the murder itself.

15c. Dark Secrets

Note that I added a dark secret to the history of Lisa Brenton, the Dentist. The reason why is that we can seem to give her a motive without really adding to the motive she already has. It is irrelevant if she is guilty, or not guilty, of the previous murder accusation. The sleuth's or suspects are here to discover who killed the current victim, and not who may, or may not have, killed someone previous to the scenario. Clever subterfuge.

I also have Claire bringing up suggestions that the Maid was stealing from the Manor, which also seems to be a dark secret for the Maid, but note that the testimony is false. If you need to give your suspects some dark secrets in their pasts that can be brought up in the scenario, the following chart may inspire you. You can determine them randomly or pick one that suits your character or story.

Chart#13 Secrets, Dirty Secrets, Crimes, Petty Crimes, and Immorality

[To use this chart you will need to generate a random number from 1 to 100. To do this you roll a D10 once for the tens number and once for the ones number. For example: I roll the D10 and the result is 5, I roll the D10 again and the result is 7 which gives me the number 57.]

D100

00-05) Theft / Extortion / Money Laundering / Burglary / Robbery / Larceny / Shop Lifting

06-09) Bribery

10-14) Manslaughter (Voluntary or Involuntary)

15-19) Drugs (Possession / Cultivation / Manufacturing / Distributing / Trafficking)

20-24) Embezzlement

25-29) Infidelity / Polygamy

30-34) Prostitution

35-39) Abortion / Adoption

40-44) Arson

45-49) Assault and Battery /Domestic Violence / Child Abuse / Hate Crime

50-54) Extortion / Blackmailing

55-59) Murder (First or Second Degree)

60-64) Fraud / Identity Theft / Tax Evasion / Insurance Fraud / Securities Fraud / Forgery

65-69) Criminal Contempt of Court

70-74) Harassment / Stalking

75-79) Perjury

80-84) Kid-napping

85-89) Conspiracy (See chart #12 Secret Societies for possible ideas)

90-94) Counterfeiting

95-99) Racketeering

So far we have created the villains' and the liars' Character Sheets, and with those out of the way, we need to create sheets for the remaining six suspects. It is a lot of work, but it will all be worth it in the end because you will have a fantastic murder mystery scenario. Your guests will rant and rave over it for the next several months and you will get all the credit, and you should, because you will be the one who did all the work. I just provided a source of inspiration, a guide, and a formula for you to follow in order to write a great murder mystery game to play with your friends, family, relatives, and neighbors.

15d. The Innocents

Keep in mind that the more suspects you wish to have in your game, the more writing you will have to do, which is why I try to keep my scenarios limited to 6-8 suspects at most, and that is pretty standard for most murder mystery games. It is up to you how much work you want to put into your scenario. If you would need more players than that, you could easily just use the Sleuth's versus Suspects variant of the game, that way you can add sleuth's to the game and have as many guests as you like. I will also explain game variants in a later chapter.

Lets continue making the character sheets for the rest of the innocent suspects. As you read these examples you will see how I linked the information and clues together to flesh out the details.

LISA BRENTON

Name: Lisa Brenton   (female)   Age: 32
Marital Status: Married

Occupation: Dentist

Areas of Expertise: Matching teeth marks to bite wounds.

Political Affiliation: Democrat

Religion: Theist

Hobbies: Reading and writing.

Habits: Addicted to breath mints. You do not smoke or drink.

Relation to the Victim: You are/were Colby Brenton's Wife.

Relations to Other Suspects: Claire Ruppel is your sister.

Guilt Status: You are innocent.

Weapon: None. It might be revealed that you could have access to a weapon.

Motive: None, but Money will be insinuated. You would receive a lot of money from that insurance policy you pulled out on Colby recently, if he were to die an untimely death.

Opportunity: As Colby's wife you would have access to keys to any room in the Manor and, of course, the ley to Colby Brenton's bed room.

Alibi: You claim to have been asleep in your room the entire night. You also claim that before going to bed, you took a heavy duty pain killer for a migraine.

Clues to Reveal: Reveal that you are married to Colby, and that Claire is your sister. You have been married four years. Reveal that you are friends with the Constable, Derryl Gramlich. After Dinner and some conversation, you may be notified by the game moderator that you have a migraine. At this point, you will tell everyone you have a migraine. Take the bottle of pills from your pocket and shake it to make a rattling noise. Tell everyone it is prescription for pain. Tell them you are going to take a pill and retire for the evening. You give your husband, Colby Brenton, a shallow hug, but you do not kiss him. You give your sister a warm hug. Tell everyone 'goodnight' and excuse yourself to your room.

Clues to Conceal: Colby is your second husband. You were married before and widowed. Your first husband, of two years, died under mysterious circumstances that will be revealed during the course of the scenario. You want to conceal your motive to commit the crime, but it would be pointless. You took out a large insurance policy on Colby Brenton a few months ago and would get a lot of money if Colby should suffer an untimely death. You want to conceal the insurance policy information.

What you know about the others:

#1: (T) Your husband, Colby Brenton, owed the Banker, Lance Gibbins, a great deal of money and he has been pestering Colby to pay up or face the consequences.

#2: (T) The Maid, Benita Lintner, has no reason to murder anyone. She is very passive and kind to everyone. She might be a little secretive, but she is honest and loyal. She once cut her hair very short and donated it. A wig was made out of it and given to a young girl that had lost her hair.

#3: (T) Erik Macha, the Barber, hated your husband, Colby Brenton, over differences in political views. You do not care much for Erik Macha, but your husband did invite him, not you.

#4: (F) Derryl Gramlich, the Constable, had absolutely no motive to kill your husband. When, and if, someone suggests he does have a motive you will debate it until you discover the truth.

During Examination of the Body: You will notice a small amount of blood in the corner of the victims mouth. It is not enough blood to gather a sample. You will see that the blood does not appear to come from any laceration, injury or cut in the victims mouth. You will keep this information to yourself until instructed by the moderator.

During Questioning: You will admit that you and your husband have been separated for quite some time, and although you still live in the Manor, you sleep in a separate room. If asked what marital issues you were having with Colby, you must reveal that his drinking and money problems were causing you both a lot of stress and heated arguments. If asked if you know, or knew, of any affairs Colby was having ,you will become a little upset and admit that you often suspected him of cheating, but never had any proof. You will be shocked and upset when it is revealed that your husband was indeed having an affair with the Fortune Teller. There will also be insinuations that Colby was having relations with the Maid, at which point, you will deny it and claim the accusation is absurd. You will state that you have total trust in Benita Lintner, that she has been a dedicated and loyal hard worker. You were the one that interviewed and hired her for the position after-all. It might be revealed that Colby was having another affair with someone very close to you. How you react is up to you. Your darkest secret may be revealed later in the game that your ex-husband died under mysterious circumstances. It is all true and you will admit that the events did take place but you will deny that you were the one that killed him. It may be revealed that the Maid was keeping secrets from you and will be apologetic. How you respond is up to you. Someone may drop a key on the floor. When they d,o try to pick it up if you can. Whether you pick it up or not, you will be able to identify the key. It is the only key that you know of that will unlock Colby Brenton's bedroom door.

ERIK MACHA

Name: Erik Macha   (male)   Age: 35

Marital Status: Single

Occupation: Barber

Areas of Expertise: (you can match hair samples)

Political Affiliation: Libertarian

Religion: Agnostic

Hobbies: You read Sherlock Holmes stories.

Habits: Pipe smoker. Light drinker.

Relation to the Victim: Acquaintance. Colby Brenton came to your Shop to get his hair cut.

Relations to Other Suspects: You are a casual acquaintance of Lance Gibbins, the Banker, you also cut his hair.

Guilt Status: You are innocent.

Weapon: None. It may be revealed you had access to the weapon or method.

Motive: Disdain. You did not like Colby Brenton concerning politics.

Opportunity: It may be revealed you had an opportunity.

Alibi: You claim to have been in your bedroom most of the night.

Clues to Reveal: You did not agree with Colby's political affiliations. Colby was a Republican who often made fun of you for being a Libertarian. If asked why you came to the party, Colby insisted you should come meet his single sister-in-law. How could you turn up free food, drinks, and the possibility of meeting a woman even if you did not like Colby? Besides, Colby tipped well and you wanted to keep his business, despite your dislike of him. Colby liked you, but you did not care for him. You have a lot of trouble sleeping in strange places. You smoke.

Clues to Conceal: You have a slight motive, you do have an opportunity and it may be suggested you had access to the weapon or method of murder. The only thing you really want to hide is that you brought some cocaine to the party, you did not realize a Constable would be present. You hid this in your room as soon as he arrived and you are nervous about it. You do not want anyone to look in your room under any circumstances. You also traffic Cocaine in the back part of your shop, if the word got out you would lose your business, and perhaps go to jail.
(Fact: Cocaine use in the U.S.A. was outlawed in 1914.)

What you know about the others:

#1: (T) Sometime after Midnight you decided to go outside for a Cigarette. As you left your room you were walking down the hall towards the staircase to the Foyer. You passed Colby Brenton's Office. The Door was half open and you saw Benita Lintner, the Maid, snooping around in the Desk as if she were searching for something. You decided it was not your business and said nothing.

#2: (T) You know that Derryl Gramlich, the Constable, has been spying on Colby Brenton and carries a concealed revolver even when he is not on duty.

#3: (T) Lance Gibbins, the Banker, told you that Colby Brenton owed him a lot of money and that he planned on getting that money back any way he had to.

#4: (F) One of your customers told you that Lisa Brenton was having an affair with a much younger man.

During Examination of the Body: You will suggest that it appears as though Colby was either choked, suffocated, or was poisoned. You will admit that you can not be certain.

During Questioning: You did not sleep well during the night. You did not like Colby Brenton, but not enough to kill him. In the middle of the night you went out to the garden for a smoke and to walk around. You saw someone smoking at the second floor Balcony, sometime after midnight, but you are not sure who it was. You think that whoever it was, may have been wearing a night gown, and perhaps it was a woman. You are not sure if the person saw you or not. You may be asked to match a hair sample found in the game. You have no issue with this and will do it gladly -it will match the hair of Lance Gibbins. You may be asked to reveal what you hid in your room and you will not want to do this, if you can, try to misdirect everyone by sharing what you know about the others. You do have an opportunity, so you will be questioned about everything that happened when you went outside to the garden for a smoke. You know it was sometime after midnight. It was dark and stormy, but the rain had died down enough for you to make it to the Gazebo in the garden. You claim the reason you wanted to go outside was for fresh air and a nice smoke. You were having a lot of trouble sleeping sleeping in such a strange place. You may say you were reflecting about the conditions of your divorce. Someone will accuse you of having a heated argument with Colby Brenton in his room sometime before dinner. You will deny the event ever took place. You will suggest that the person is mistaken and that it could have been Lance Gibbins, the Banker. You will still be very nervous about the drugs hidden in your room.

DERRYL GRAMLICH

Name: Derryl Gramlich   (male)   Age: 45

Marital Status: Married

Occupation: Constable

Areas of Expertise: You specialize in Ballistics. You can identify gunshot residue. You can match bullets to firearms. You can identify gunshot wounds and match them to firearms.

Political Affiliation: Communist

Religion: Atheist

Hobbies: None

Habits: Pipe smoker. Trouble sleeping.

Relation to the Victim: Acquaintance.

Relations to Other Suspects: You are married to Madame Edwina, the Fortune Teller. You are friends with Lisa Brenton, the Dentist, she invited you and she is Colby's wife.

Guilt Status: You are innocent! Mostly.

Weapon: You may have had access to the weapon or method for murder.

Motive: Colby Brenton was having an affair with your wife and you know it.

Opportunity: You may, or may not have, had an opportunity to commit the crime.

Alibi: You claim to have slept through the entire night.

Clues to Reveal: You are friends with Colby's wife, Lisa Brenton, the Dentist. You were invited by Lisa.You claim to take medication which helps you sleep. You took one of these before retiring to your bedroom for the night. You claim you are allergic to the smell of the smoke from the Clove cigarettes your wife smokes. When she smokes you always nag her to quit.

Clues to Conceal: Your wife was having an affair with Colby Brenton, and you are very embarrassed about this because you feel this reflects poorly on your image as a man. You wrote a threat note to Colby Brenton demanding he end the affair, and that if he did not, you would make him suffer for it. You do not want anyone to know about this note for several reasons. The note would implicate you as the possible villain. The threat could get you in some trouble at your place of employment with the Constabulary Station, as it would be considered harassment. You spied on your wife and Colby Brenton to establish that the affair was true. You do not want your wife to know that you know. You are hoping to work things out with her because you love her. You have never confronted her about it. You are secretly involved with the Communist Political Party and you do not want anyone to find out, as it could really hurt your career in law enforcement. You keep a concealed pistol with you off duty in case of emergencies.

What you know about the others:

#1: (T) Lisa Brenton, the Dentist, was once accused of murdering her ex-husband but she was never convicted in court. Her ex-husband was smothered to death with a pillow.

#2: (T) Colby Brenton owed Lance Gibbins, the Banker, a lot of money and Lance Gibbins intended to sue him in court, or take other drastic measures to collect on this debt.

#3: (T) You saw Claire Ruppel, the Beautician, sneak into Colby Brenton's room on your way to your bedroom. You thought it was suspicious, but decided it was not your business.

#4: (F) You claim you saw Colby Brenton and Benita Lintner, the Maid, having a private and hushed argument shortly before dinner and Colby slapped her hard across her face. You decided it was not your business and said nothing about it. You think it occurred around 4:35 PM.

During Examination of the Body: You will be able to determine that Colby Brenton was not shot, stabbed, or killed by blunt trauma as there are no obvious wounds on the body. You reason he could have been poisoned or perhaps suffocated somehow. You will notice recent gunshot residue on Colby Brenton's right hand. You will then tell everyone that Colby used a handgun of some kind at some time during the night. You will search Colby's body for handgun and not find one. You will let everyone know that you are investigating the Billiard Room. After awhile, you will tell everyone that Colby could not have been murdered in this room. If asked why, you will state that Colby fired a gun, but there is no gun in this room, nor is there a bullet or a bullet hole anywhere. You will suggest the next best place to investigate would be Colby's bedroom. You will not find the note in the back pocket of Colby's pants.

During Questioning: You may be accused of being involved with the Communist Political Party and involved in some secret conspiracy and you will deny it. You will notice Erik Macha, the Barber, acting suspicious and you will wonder why. You might ask him why he seems nervous. Eventually you will learn why, and you will want to investigate the matter. Someone may reveal that a suspect was snooping around Colby's Office, and this will interest you very much and suggest that it may be relevant to the motive of the killer. Someone may suggest your wife was having an affair and you will try to cover for her. Someone may accuse you of having written a threat note to Colby Brenton, and you did. You can try to deny it, but someone may try to match the handwriting on the note to the notes you have been taking in your note book. At first you will use your position as an officer of the law to refuse to submitting your note book as evidence. Remember that your wife could easily identify your handwriting style, or match a fingerprint on the note to your hand. You will use everything that you know about the others to misdirect the suspicion on you. If someone states that you are lying about something, you will always respond with the following:

"I am an Officer of the Law and I do not lie! You have no authority to question my honesty."

Notice how I used Derryl Gramlich's Political Affiliation as a Dirty Secret in his character sheet. You can use anything you want to cast suspicion on the suspects of your stories. Also note how I did not think that Erik Macha was suspicious enough and gave him a dirty secret involving drugs. He will not want that information revealed and will act suspicious during the course of the game as it unfolds. This will make the other suspects wonder what he is hiding, as it might be relevant to the plot. The reason he will want to hide this is because a Constable is present.

Aside from physical clues and evidence, in a murder mystery, you can use almost anything from political affiliations, religious beliefs, dirty secrets, petty crimes, habits, and perhaps even good deeds as non-physical clues to link a suspect to a weapon, motive, opportunity or a lack of a solid alibi. It would even be interesting if you could use someone's dirty secret as their alibi. Be creative and use your imagination.

BENITA LINTNER

Name: Benita Lintner   (female)   Age: 33

Marital Status: Single

Occupation: Maid / House Keeper

Areas of Expertise: You can match dust samples and carpet fiber samples.

Political Affiliation: Un-affiliated.

Religion: Theist.

Hobbies: Does gambling count?

Habits: Casual drinker and social smoker.

Relation to the Victim: You worked for Colby Brenton at the Manor.

Relations to Other Suspects: You worked for Lisa Brenton, the Dentist, at the Manor. You would be acquainted with Nelson Brenton, the Tobacconist.

Guilt Status: You are innocent.

Weapon: You have access to the method or weapon used to commit the crime.

Motive: You have no motive.

Opportunity: You had a definite opportunity to commit the crime.

Alibi: You do not have a solid alibi. You did not go to bed until sometime around 12:40 AM

Clues to Reveal: You will reveal your relation to Colby and Lisa Brenton as your employers. You will reveal you have been working for them a long time. You like to gamble. You also work part-time as a waitress for a local diner. You do not like Nelson Brenton. You are polite to him only because you work for the Brentons. He often makes snide remarks to you and this annoys you and you will make it clear that you do not appreciate it. You smoke socially. If, and only if, someone asks you if you had an argument with Colby the day before, deny it was an argument. You did have a private conversation, but not an argument, Colby told you he had plans to end the affair with Madame Edwina, but try to keep this a secret as long as possible.

Clues to Conceal: You are not aware of the key hidden in your pocket. Someone planted it on you. You are not who you claim to be. Benita Lintner is not your real name. You are not only an illegal immigrant, but you are also wanted by Law Enforcement for Identity Theft Charges, Forgery, and Conning several men you dated out of large sums of money, which you squandered on gambling. Your real name is Evette Dupont. You do not want anyone to learn your true Identity. Colby found out about your real name, and your true identity, but knew nothing of your darker secrets other than your status as an illegal immigrant. If the Constable finds out who you really are, you will be in a lot of trouble and possibly be deported back to France where you are wanted for even deeper darker secrets that you will never confess to.

What you know about the others:

#1:(T) Nelson Brenton, the Tobacconist, would have a reason to want Colby dead, as he would inherit the Estate and the Manor. You make it clear that you do not like him and suggest that he could be the culprit.

#2:(T) You saw Madame Edwina, the Fortune Teller, smoking on the balcony while you were puttering around the Manor late at night.

#3:(T) You saw Erik Macha, the Barber, coming inside the back door of the Manor from the garden sometime after Midnight. You also saw him hiding something suspicious in his room before dinner last night.

#4:(F) Claire Ruppel, the Beautician, was embezzling money from the Estate trust accounts.

During Examination of the Body: You will notice the dust on Colby Brenton's clothing. You will suggest it is similar to the dust found in his room and that it does not seem to match the dust of the Billiard room. Someone may point out that you have dust on your uniform also. When this happens say something like:

'So what about the dust? I'm the Maid, I clean and dust here all day, there are any number of ways I could have gotten this dust on me. The dust you see on Colby's clothing matches the dust found in his room. I do clean his room occasionally as well as you might imagine, it is my job after-all.'

During Questioning: You admit to having access to all they keys and rooms in the Manor. You will reveal that you were up late cleaning-up after the guests. You must reveal your lack of a solid alibi. You have been keeping secrets from Lisa Brenton. If someone asks if you were taking bribes from Colby Brenton to keep quiet about his affairs, you will confess that it is true and that you really needed the extra money. Colby is dead, there is no more point in covering for him anymore. You will act very embarrassed, hang your head down in shame, you will be very apologetic to Lisa Brenton, the Dentist, about this. You have felt guilty about this for a long time. You will want to give Lisa a hug. At some point someone will suggest that you have access to the keys of the manor, when they do you just say:

'I do have access to all the keys of the Mansion, do I need remind you that I work here?'.

After that, the Key in your pocket falls to the floor, it is the only key that will unlock Colby Brenton's room. You will act surprised and claim that you do not know how it got there. Someone may ask why you were snooping around Colby's office. You were making sure Colby had not left out any information about your true identity that the Constable might find.

LANCE GIBBINS

Name: Lance Gibbins   (male)   Age: 55

Marital Status: Married

Occupation: Banker

Areas of Expertise: (you can match handwriting samples)

Political Affiliation: Freemason

Religion: Theist (Supreme Being)

Hobbies: You like to play the Stock Market.

Habits: You smoke cigars and drink.

Relation to the Victim: Acquaintance

Relations to Other Suspects: You are a casual acquaintance of the Barber, Erik Macha, he cuts your hair.

Guilt Status: You are innocent.

Weapon: It may be revealed you had access to a weapon or method of murder.

Motive: Colby Brenton owed you a lot of money.

Opportunity: It may be revealed you had an opportunity.

Alibi: You claim to have been sleeping in your room the entire night.

Clues to Reveal: You will reveal that you have been invited to the party by Lisa Brenton, but your reason for accepting the invitation was to discuss business matters with the Brenton family. You are a casual acquaintance of the Barber, Erik Macha, he cuts your hair.

Clues to Conceal: Colby Brenton owed you a large amount of money. He has been avoiding paying you anything at all on his debt and you were tired of it, you came to the party with intentions of collecting the money by putting some pressure on Colby. You had an heated argument with Colby in his bedroom before dinner at around 4:45PM. The conversation lasted between ten and fifteen minutes at most.

What you know about the others:

#1: (T) You saw Erik Macha, the Barber, hiding something in his room, shortly after the Constable arrived.

#2: (T) Erik Macha, the Barber, disliked Colby Brenton over differences of opinion concerning politics.

#3: (T) Benita Lintner, the Maid, often cashed checks at your bank with a questionable Identity Card. You could never prove the document was false or had any reason to believe the checks were fraudulent. All of them cleared, however, you suspect she is not who she claims to be.

#4: (F) Nelson Brenton, the Tobacconist, was embezzling money from the Estate trust accounts.

During Examination of the Body: You have no experience in the observation of such matters. You will cover your mouth with a cloth hankerchief as you look at the corpse of Colby Brenton.

You will say that the body is starting to smell. You will stand out of the way and let the others examine the body.

During Questioning: You may be asked if you had an argument with Colby, in his bedroom, before dinner last night. You will deny it was an argument and claim it was a business discussion. Someone may suggest that Brenton owed you a lot of money and you will confirm that fact. If pressed on the matter, you will be forced to admit that the discussion turned heated.

Colby got mad and pushed you into the chair in his room. You will then state that this angered you, but that an altercation was not going to solve the matter. You then told Colby you would see him in Court to settle the debt. You left his room intending to leave for the night, but Lisa Brenton convinced you to stay for dinner and that she would talk to Colby about paying up on the debt as soon as possible. This placated you and you decided to stay the remainder of the night. Ask Madame Edwina to show everyone the broken pocket watch clue and reveal it's time.

You may be asked to match the handwriting of a note to another suspects handwriting style and you will have no issue with this. If you are given the opportunity to observe the Constables note book, you will notice it matches the writing style on the note. Someone might try to match a clue to you and you will not resist. You have nothing to hide.

NELSON BRENTON

Name: Nelson Brenton   (male)   Age: 29

Marital Status: Divorced / Single

Occupation: Tobacconist

Areas of Expertise: (you can match tobacco and ash samples)

Political Affiliation: Democrat

Religion: Theist

Hobbies: You collect coins and stamps.

Habits: Pipe smoker. Light drinker.

Relation to the Victim: You are Colby Brenton's younger brother.

Relations to Other Suspects: You are Lisa Brenton's brother-in-law.

Guilt Status: You are innocent.

Weapon: It may be implied you could have had access to a weapon.

Motive: Money. You would most likely inherit the Manor and the Estate if Colby died.

Opportunity: It may be revealed you could have had an opportunity.

Alibi: You claim to have been sleeping in your room all night.

Clues to Reveal: Establish with guests your relation to Colby, Lisa, and Claire Ruppel. You are not all about money at all. You feel the simpler things in life are much better than money. You enjoy Jazz music and often went to see your brother perform at the local venues. You have always been supportive of his talents and dreams, but have always been disappointed about your brothers drinking problem and bad money management skills. You do not care much for the Maid, Benita Lintner, you always felt like she was hiding something.

Clues to Conceal: You knew your brother was a cheater and it disgusted you, but you said nothing to keep the peace in the family. You often argued with Colby about his lecherous activities. You do not like the Maid because she would not date you. You really do not have much to hide.

What you know about the others:

#1:(T) Derryl Gramlich, the Constable, is a Communist and has been hiding it for a long time.

#2:(T) Madame Edwina has been visiting Colby Brenton at the Manor a lot lately. Sometimes late at night. She has stayed the night a few times.

#3:(T) Benita Lintner, the Maid, is not who she claims to be. You will suggest that she is hiding something and could be the culprit.

#4:(F) Claire Ruppel, the Beautician, had access to various poisons such as arsenic and cyanide.

During Examination of the Body: You are upset. You are not a crime scene investigator and decide to stay out of the way while the others investigate the body. After they are done, you will notice the piece of paper in the back pocket of your brothers body. You will take it, and read it, then fold it up and place it in your vest pocket. You decide it is too personal to reveal what it says to everyone else and refuse to let anyone look at it. You will not bring it up again until someone starts making some interesting suggestions about the Constable. When prompted by the moderator, you will take the note from your pocket and show it to the Banker, and then after he has read it, ask him to show it to Madame Edwina.

During Questioning: You may be asked about your motive. There is no point in denying that you are now the most likely heir to the Manor and the Estate, but you will claim you had no motive to kill your brother because Colby has squandered away a large portion of the family's money. Everyone will want to know why you are concealing the letter and you will reassure them that it is very personal and the information it contains is very sensitive. You will deny accusations that you were embezzling money from the Estate. You were one of the last people to see Colby alive, as you were the one who helped Colby make it to his bedroom for the night. At 11:25PM Colby was so drunk he could not walk a straight line. You escorted him to his bedroom, helped him take off his suit jacket and shoes. Colby plopped down on to the bed and passed out. You closed the door on your way out, but did not lock it.

Finally, all the suspects character sheets are written, at least for the most part. Now we should go back and fill in all the details that we may have had to skip until all the character sheets were completed. It is much easier and far more logical to write some of this information in for the character sheets when we have a clear understanding of the story we are writing, and after we know all of the suspects general information.

At this point, if you have not done so already, complete all the steps that you may have skipped. Establish each characters Relation to Victim, Relation to Other Suspects, Clues to Reveal, Clues to Conceal, What they know about the others, During Examination of the Body, and During

Questioning. The following sub-chapters describe how to do this, except for the 'What you know about the others' which I will describe in the following chapter (Chapter 16).

15e. Relation to the Victim.

None of the suspects have to be related to the victim. For the purposes of the story, however, we might wish to have a few suspects who are somehow related to the victim in question. It all may depend on the type of scenario you are writing for your murder mystery. There are several ways that a suspect can be related to the victim without being in the family.

In the notes for the suspects, we use the word 'Relation' as more of a term to describe how each particular suspect knows the victim or the others. It is possible that a suspect does not really know the victim at all, but typically in a murder mystery scenario we probably want all of the suspects to know the victim in some way that will be relevant to the plot of the story. Here is a list of possible relations. You should probably select this information as opposed to randomly determining it, but if you do need to randomly determine the information, I have the chart set up so that you may do so.

Chart#14 Relation to Victim

D20	(cont.)	Chart#15 Relative Type
		D10
1) Relative (see chart#15)	11) Ex-Friend	1) Parent / Guardian
2) Friend	12) Ex-Employee	2) Sibling
3) Associate	13) Ex-Employer	3) Aunt / Uncle
4) Spouse / Partner	14) Coworker	4) Cousin
5) Casual Lovers	15) Acquaintance	5) Child
6) Casual Acquaintance	16) Business Partner	6) In-Law
7) Employee	17) Client	7) God-Parent
8) Employer	18) Secret Lover	8) Step-Parent
9) Ex-Lover	19) Friend	9) Step-Child
10) Ex-Spouse	20) Relative (see chart#15)	10) God-Child

15f. Relation to Other Suspects.

None of the suspects have to be related to each other either, but for the purposes of the story, you might want to establish some sort of relation between suspects if it should be relevant to your story. If not, you may have to wonder how it is that the suspects would know anything at all about each other, and therefore how they could reveal any useful information during the course of the murder mystery game story. For example, it would not be fair or make any sense, if the Mail Man were to accuse the Milk Man of having an affair with the victims wife, if they have never even met before. You can select the relation from Chart#14, on the previous page, or determine it randomly.

15g. Clues to Reveal and Clues to Conceal.

Clues to reveal or conceal usually involve the information each suspect knows about themselves and how it might be relevant to the murder mystery scenario. Many of the suspects may have dirty secrets to hide or some other information that might make them look innocent or guilty. We will use this information to drop some very vague hints throughout the game that may, or may not, support some ones suspicion in the overall scenario.

By reviewing the example character sheets, you should be able to see my point. Each suspect might reveal information which they may feel is safe to divulge whether it pertains to themselves, or to someone else. For example, in Madame Edwina's character sheet, I noted that she would reveal that she is lonely a lot of the time because her husband works so much. This is a very vague hint into her character and to the fact that she is having an affair to soothe her loneliness. It is the perfect clue for her to reveal because it helps tell a story about this character and her dirty secret without actually giving away any hint into her motivation or the solution to the mystery. Besides all that, at the time she reveals this information, she does not have any plans to kill anyone just yet, so there would be no reason for her to conceal such information.

Note that Madame Edwina must also reveal that her husband is a deep sleeper. This is a clever hint that many of the others might not even pay any attention to when she says it. It is a vague hint that she will have an opportunity to commit the crime, but only if it is validated that her husband is in fact a deep sleeper. It might seem too much information, especially when her husband reveals that he takes medication which helps him sleep, but there is no way for the other suspects or sleuth's to establish whether he will actually take the medication or not.

They must remember they could be getting set up with false information for two different reasons. One of those reasons being is that everyone knows there is a liar amongst them. The liar could easily be Edwina, or her husband Derryl. The other reason is that the information might not be any hint about Edwina herself, but that it might be a hint into the possibility that Derryl too could also later have an opportunity.

Be both clever and careful when writing your clues to reveal and clues to conceal information. Use these to help tell the story, to develop character, and to possibly drop some hints that will sway the story in favor of your murder mystery story.

Here is another example worth noting, Lisa is the first to go to bed and reveals that she has a migraine for which she will take medication. The other suspects, and/or sleuth's, will be wondering if this is important or not. Does she really have a migraine? They can not know. Does she in fact have medication for migraines? Yes she does. Will she actually take those pills? They can not be sure. For all they know she is establishing an alibi for herself before the crime occurs.

15h. During Examination of the Body.

Each suspect may, or may not, find certain clues once they have been presented, or located the victims body. We have already established that each suspect has an area of expertise which will help guide us in deciding who could make sense of the clues found. It was not necessary to have the Barber be the one to find the hair clue, nor was it necessary for the Beautician to find the lipstick smudge clues. For example, I had Madame Edwina be the suspect to notice the dust clue, even though she has no way to compare dust samples. Edwina does not get to collect the clue, but does get to suggest it makes the Maid look suspicious.

The Maid can, but then why should she say anything about such a clue if she feels it might make her look suspicious? This is why the Maid will find the dust clue, now she is forced to hold the only clue that links her to the crime and at some point she may have to confess that the dust on Colby's body and his room do in fact match the dust on her own uniform.

I wanted the Constable to find the gunshot residue clue because he is the only suspect who would even think of looking for such a clue to begin with. Gunshot residue is not really visible to the naked eye and usually requires a special kit to find it, but we step a little into the fantastical and let the Constable discover it anyways. It would not make any sense for the Barber to find that clue and present it to the Constable for examination. A bullet on the other hand, anyone might notice that, and think it was a relevant clue. Remember, be creative, clever, and careful when determining who should find each clue or clues.

We will also want to describe here, how each character might act when they see the corpse of the victim. Obviously those who are closest to the victim should be very upset, unless they are themselves uncaring, or simply a cold blooded killer. I thought Lisa and Nelson would be the most upset upon finding out Colby has been murdered. Some suspects might be rather indifferent, which could make them look guilty.

The Banker would also be upset, but primarily because he might not ever see the money he is owed now. While I am on the subject, note that the Banker's motive for killing Colby Brenton might also serve as his possible alibi. Sure, he has a motive for murder because Colby owed him a lot of money and was slacking on paying it back, but if he kills Colby, who will pay him back now? Cleverly hidden in the Banker's motive is also his alibi.

15i. Hobbies & Habits

Need to decide what kind of Hobbies and Habits a character might have? Here are some ideas. Sometimes in a murder mystery a suspects habits and hobbies could provide clues that could be found in the scenario. For example, in real life sometimes a killer is a smoker and leaves a cigarette at the scene of the crime, which is a clue used by investigators to identify the killer. This persons habit helped them get caught. The same could happen in the case of a killer whose hobby is collecting rare and/or unusual coins. If they happened to drop such a coin at the scene of the crime, this type of clue could help investigators narrow down the number of possible suspects based on their hobbies.

The following chart is very basic to say the least. For more ideas use the Internet to search for 'list of habits' or 'list of hobbies' as there is not enough room in this book to encompass all of the possibilities. This list is provided as nothing more than a starting point for more research if you need more ideas than what I have provided. Note that I only include a simple list because the hobbies and habits of any particular character are not the central focus of a murder mystery, but could add depth to the characters and allow for some improvisational personality quirks and dialogue. We do want the characters to have something to talk about during casual conversation. If you do not need any of these then lets move on to the next chapter and decide who knows what about who.

Chart# 16 Habits	Chart#17 Hobbies
D20	D20
1) Nail Biting	1) Gambling
2) Smoker	2) Dancing
3) Drinker	3) Stamp Collector
4) Complaining	4) Coin Collector
5) Drug use	5) Singing
6) Chews Gum	6) Plays Musical Instrument
7) Itching	7) Sewing / Needle Craft
8) Interrupting	8) Reading
9) Talks to self	9) Sports
10) Sweets/Candy	10) Fencing
11) Staring	11) Geology
12) Not listening	12) Writing
13) Being rude	13) Games
14) Laughing loudly	14) Movies
15) Pointing	15) Music
16) Flirting	16) Bird Watching
17) Giggly	17) Arts
18) Asks too many questions	18) Puzzles
19) Mumbling	19) Astronomy
20) Talks too much	20) Gardening

16. WHO KNOWS WHAT ABOUT WHO?

All of the suspect sheets are now nearly complete. You may be puzzled how to determine who is going to know what about who. The best thing to do, as mentioned earlier, is to create and complete all of your suspects sheets first, but skipping what they know about each other until the very last. Then go back and fill in that information with what you now know about all of your suspects. This information will become their testimonies during the investigation and questioning stage of the game.

They each will know, or think they know, at least four things. Remember that the villain will know two true pieces of information and two false. The liar will only know one true piece of information, and three false. Everyone else will tell three pieces of true information, and only one false. In total that is 32 statements, 21 of which will be true, and 11 of which will be false.

Fill in all the true pieces of information for each suspect first. The most important thing to do is to make sure that at least half of the innocent suspects hint to something that might shed light on the villains sinister deed whether it be their access to a weapon, motive or an opportunity.

If it is possible, make one innocent reveal something about the killers possible motive. Have one suspect reveal the killers access to a weapon, and one suspect could know about the killers opportunity and thus lack of a legitimate alibi. Have at least one suspect tell a lie about the villain, even if it means they are vouching for them in some way. Thus there would be three suspects revealing something true about the villain, and one suspect telling a lie about them.

If players were keeping count as to who is being talked about the most, it could be a dead give away who the villain is, so make sure at least three other suspects have four pieces of testimony being witnessed against them also, whether it is true or false. With the rest of the suspects information try to get them pointing fingers at each-other.

This information they know could either suggest access to a weapon, a motive, an opportunity or an alibi. For the most part, I use suspect testimony to try and reveal the real motives or the implied possible motives of the other suspects and to reveal subplot stories that might have developed. I also use these to have the characters dig up and reveal dirty secrets and possibly even past good deeds about the others. Reason being is that the clues and red herrings that will be found, typical, already suggest or imply the suspects possible opportunities. Those clues may also already imply access to a weapon also. So, in most cases, use testimony to reveal motives and to make suspects look like they are possibly guilty somehow.

When the suspects are discussing the case, and questioning each other, we want to create some tension in their interactions. Some suspects might be vouching for others. Also try to use the true information that they share to cleverly reveal pieces of the plot without giving it directly away.

The point is to get them talking, interacting, and forcing each other to reveal more and more about themselves and what they may, or may not know, about the others. By doing this, there will be debates, arguments, agreements, and maybe accusations. It will also create dialogue that will help tell the story. These interactions will become quite memorable for all the players.

For me, the most challenging part is writing the false testimonies that the characters will reveal. Use false testimony to cast suspicion on those who clearly seem to shine the most as possible innocents. It would seem that using false information in this way would be counter productive, but it really is not. These false pieces of information, as they are revealed, will force the suspects to use logic and reason to try and separate the facts and fictions of any persons testimony, and it will also prompt them to interact with each other in such a way as to question and re-question valuable information. Not only that, the false pieces of information once again serve as plot devices and red herrings.

No witness is ever completely accurate when giving testimony. People are often prone to believing the rumors and gossip that they hear and sometimes even accepting their personal opinions and perceptions of another person as fact, even if there is no validation. Use your imagination, reason, and logic.

In the example I wrote, no one could possibly know that Madame Edwina had any motive, because she did not have one at all, until the last moment. Therefore I had to have suspects share information that would reveal that she definitely had an opportunity despite her alleged alibi and catch her in a lie. In my example, the only two people who could possibly know Edwina's motive are Colby and Edwina herself. The suspects may be able to figure out her motive if they happen to ask Benita Lintner a very important question, but there is no way she can confirm Colby ever followed through with what he related to the Maid in their private discussion the night before.

Almost anyone could have had access to the pillow at some point, but the Maid will seem the most likely to have access. Through testimony and careful examination of the clues and evidence, the suspects should be able to gather that Madame Edwina definitely had contact with Colby after he went to bed, and was in fact in his room some time during the night. Remember that two legitimate clues place her in Colby's room.

They may not ever be able to establish her identity as the killer, but the evidence will make her look guilty enough, especially when the Dentist has an epiphany, and suggests that Colby Brenton bit his assailant. The moderator may have to prompt her to come to this conclusion at some point in the story, probably when the solution is revealed. This would be done after the votes have been counted, to make a great ending for the finale of the story and end to the game.

I will discuss more ideas about methods for ending and concluding the game scenario in a later chapter. For now, lets move on to creating a time line of events that we will be able to refer to when deciding how the game scenario should be played out from beginning to end.

17. CREATING THE TIME LINE

For suspects to make any sense of exactly what happens during the scenario, we need to be sure certain pieces of information are revealed at the appropriate times. As host and moderator, we also need to be completely sure that we know the time line of events from the beginning of the scenario up until the final conclusion is revealed and the game is ended. We do not want to leave an important or crucial event out of the story.

If we do not have an accurate time line, the scenario will become muddled and confusing. This goes back to our earlier discussion that every story must have a beginning, middle, and an end. So, how does the story begin? Using my example, I can already establish a certain chain of events that must happen in order to tell the story. Here is the basic list of events that I will start with and then fill in the details. Eventually I will want to establish times of the day or night for each event.

- Guests arrive sometime afternoon, probably after lunch.
- Guests introduce themselves and get casually acquainted to each-other.
- Moderator explains which rooms in their home (or wherever) represent important areas relevant to the game. Gives them each a map if necessary.
- As Colby, moderator greets the guests and explains who will be sleeping where.
- Guests are given some time to interact and complete certain objectives.
- As Colby, moderator announces dinner.
- The guests meet in the dining room, have dinner, and continue getting more acquainted with each-other.
- As Colby, the moderator reveals necessary information about Colby's character, persona, and relation to each of the guests. Some general story plot could be revealed here as necessary. Certain characters may reveal some information about themselves that may be important to the plot.
- Dinner will conclude and the party will move to the lounge for drinks and conversation.

- Guests are given time to interact with each other and Colby for a short duration. Certain plot information and character information might get revealed here through the characters objectives.

- Colby and Guests eventually retire to their rooms for the night in a certain order to reveal important plot information.

- Moderator announces that the night passes and turns into morning.

- As the Butler, the moderator introduces himself to the guests.

- Moderator announces Colby's death and announces that some one killed him.

- Moderator shows the suspects to the place of Colby's corpse.

- Moderator gives private notes to each character revealing what they may gather from the scene.

- Moderator announces that the game is afoot and that they may start investigating the crime and questioning each-other.

- The suspects and or sleuth`s will learn about the real crime scene and want to investigate Colby's bedroom.

- Moderator explains the door to Colby's Bedroom is locked.

- After the key is located the investigation may continue.

- Moderator plays referee if necessary and may answer certain questions privately as needed.

- Suspects are given a certain time limit to investigate, gather clues, evaluate evidence and question each-other. Maybe an hour.

- After the time limit has been reached or it seems the investigation is reaching some sort of a conclusion the moderator announces that time is up.

- Moderator ends the game however they see fit based on the events that transpired.

That appears to be the general chain of events that should take place from the beginning of the game and the story up until the final conclusion where the solution may be revealed after a vote. The game events sequence and the story time line will be slightly different.

To create the story line I need to review all my scenario notes, and the character sheets, to establish a detailed chronological order of events for my reference during the game as it plays out. This will help me reveal story information and prompt players as necessary to take certain actions or reveal critical character information as needed. Here is the story scenario time line as it applies to my murder mystery game example.

8/10/22 Day / Night of the Dinner Party.

2:00PM Guests start Arriving one by one.

3:00PM Erik Macha hides something in his bedroom.

4:35PM An alleged argument takes place between Colby and the Maid.

4:45PM An argument occurred in Colby's bedroom between Colby and the Banker.

5:00PM Lance Gibbins left Colby's room.

7:00PM Dinner was served.

8:30PM Drinks and Conversation in the Lounge.

10:45PM Lisa Brenton went to bed first.

11:25PM Nelson Brenton helped Colby to his bedroom.

11:30PM Guests started retiring to their rooms.

11:45PM Claire Ruppel visited with Colby in his room.

8/11/22 It is a new day.

12:03AM-12:08AM Maid snooping around Colby's Office.

12:05AM Erik Macha went out to the garden for a cigarette.

12:15AM Edwina woke up.

12:30AM Edwina visits Colby's room.

12:35AM Erik came inside from the Garden.

12:40AM Benita went to bed.

12;40AM Erik Macha went to bed.

12:40AM Edwina and Colby talk.

12:45AM Colby murdered.

8:00AM Everyone wakes up, the Body is found, and the Murder is announced.

18. THE BEGINNING, MIDDLE, AND END

With the time line complete, I can be sure to direct the story and game in a logical order. Now that I have the entire beginning planned, it will be easy to write it into a story. All of the above events lead up to the middle of the story, which is where the live action and role-playing will take place.

The middle of the story, therefore, is sort of made up as we go, but we do know the key elements of the story will be unfolded for this part. The suspects will examine the body. They will find clues. They will begin to question each-other and investigate the actual crime scene when it is found. All of that will make the middle of the story and game.

The end will come either when the investigation time limit runs out, or when it appears the suspects have gathered enough clues, evidence and testimony to start reaching a likely conclusion. For the middle part of the game to run smoothly, the players will need to know their rules for the game and they will need to know what information they can gather from the investigation. Before we discuss the player rules, lets establish what all players should know at each stage of the game and story, and how you will run the event.

18a. The Beginning

The beginning of the game will be called Act#1 and will reveal the first part of the story. Each Act may be broken down into however many stages that you might need to tell the story and to let characters perform actions and complete objectives which will also help tell the story and perhaps provide a few hints.

- Guests will show up in costume with some safe information about their characters, what they know about the scenario, and themselves. They should just reveal their names at this point. This is also a good time to let your guests get their real life general chit chat out of the way.

Example: Here is the 'safe' information Madame Edwina, the Fortune Teller, should receive when I invite this player.

MADAME EDWINA

Brenton Manor, Manitou Springs, Colorado ,1922

Dear Edwina, you have been invited to a special occasion at Brenton Manor. Colby Brenton is having a Celebration Dinner Party and would like for you to attend.

Name: Madame Edwina   (female)   Age: 42

Marital Status: Married

Occupation: Psychic Consultant and Fortune Teller

Areas of Expertise: Insight, knowledge, matching fingerprint/handprint samples.

Political Affiliation: Un-affiliated

Religion: Metaphysical Spirituality

Costume Suggestions: Colorful gypsy and nomad style clothing or metaphysical apparel. Fancy costume jewelry, lots of make-up, a veil or fancy head-dress. Black boots and stockings.

Props: You smoke Clove cigarettes. You do not have to smoke a real cigarette, perhaps a fake one or a real one that is not even lit. Cigarette wand. Tarot Deck, a pack of playing cards is fine. Pack of cigarettes.

Acting Advice: You play a mysterious Fortune Teller and Palm Reader, perhaps you have a deck of Tarot cards handy in your purse. Your physical actions might be slow and languid. You are a quiet sort, listening to everyone else, before putting your two cents in about the spiritual, metaphysical, paranormal and occult aspects of any particular conversation. You like to mystify people with your words, your persona and style. You are a smoker and perhaps you have a cigarette wand. Maybe you want to read someone's palm at the party. You always ask people about their Astrology sign like this: *"What is your Sign darling?"*

Relation to the Victim: You are an acquaintance of Colby Brenton, he is fascinated with Astrology and Tarot and he often consults with you for advice concerning love and money.

Relations to Other Suspects: You are married to the Constable, Derryl Gramlich. The two of you have an unusual marriage. Derryl works a lot and you run a small Psychic Consultation business.

When all guests have arrived...

- The moderator will announce that the game has begun. Everyone should leave their real persona's behind now and become their characters.
- The moderator will discuss one more time why they are all here and explain the premise of the story.
- Players perform their Character Objectives for Stage#1 as explained on their character sheets.
- All stages, events and actions that must be performed up until the victim is found dead should be played out. This may include conversations, actions or objectives before and after Dinner, dessert, and perhaps drinks.

18b. The Middle

ACT#2

- The moderator leads the characters to the body and describes any information on how the body was found. Players are given the information they need to know while investigating the location of the body. Perhaps give this information to them in an envelope and allow them some time to read it privately. You could also use props to represent the clues that could be found and just assign the clues to the suspects that you think should find each clue as described in Chapter 13a.

Example: Here is the information that I would give to Claire Ruppel.

<u>During Examination of the Body</u>: You will notice the lipstick smudges on Colby Brenton's shirt collar, but say nothing about them, you already know one of them is yours and it might incriminate you and reveal your dark secret. You do not think the other smudge is so suspicious as you realize it could be your sisters. You will notice some Dust on the victims clothing and point it out. You will notice there are no physical bruises or markings on the body and suggest that Colby may have been poisoned.

- The characters are allowed to investigate the body and ask questions to the moderator as needed.

- The moderator announces that the real game is afoot now and they are allowed to begin their investigation to gather clues and testimony from each other. Here you would give them the rest of their information. Clues to reveal, clues to conceal, what they know about each other and how to act and or react during questioning.

Give this to them in an envelope and allow them some time to read it privately. Perhaps you will allow them to be seated for the most part somewhere in your home, like the living room, while they read their notes. When they are ready, have the suspects pair up to question each other one at a time privately in separate rooms if possible. Let them alternate until everyone has had a chance to talk with the suspects they want to. Let them know their time limit if any. When time is getting close to running out, announce how much time they have left and tell them to wrap up their investigations.

Here is an example of the information that might be given to Nelson Brenton.

Alibi: You claim to have been sleeping in your room all night.

Clues to Reveal: Establish with guests your relation to Colby, Lisa and Claire Ruppel. You are not all about money at all. You feel the simpler things in life are much better than money. You enjoy Jazz music and often went to see your brother perform at the local venues. You have always been supportive of his talents and dreams, but have always been disappointed about your brothers drinking problem and bad money management skills. You do not care much for the Maid, Benita Lintner, you always felt like she was hiding something.

Clues to Conceal: You knew your brother was a cheater and it disgusted you, but you said nothing to keep the peace in the family. You often argued with Colby about his lecherous activities. You do not like the Maid because she would not date you. You really do not have much to hide.

What you know about the others:

#1: Derryl Gramlich, the Constable, is a Communist and has been hiding it for a long time.

#2: Madame Edwina has been visiting Colby Brenton at the Manor a lot lately. Sometimes late at night. She has stayed the night a few times.

#3: Benita Lintner, the Maid, is not who she claims to be. You will suggest that she is hiding something and could be the culprit.

#4: Claire Ruppel, the Beautician, has access to various poisons such as arsenic and cyanide.

During Questioning: You may be asked about your motive. There is no point in denying that you are now the most likely heir to the Manor and the Estate, but you will claim you had no motive to kill your brother because Colby has squandered away a large portion of the family's money. Everyone will want to know why you are concealing the letter and you will reassure them that it is personal and the information it contains is very sensitive. You will deny accusations that you were embezzling money from the Estate. You were one of the last people to see Colby alive, as you were the one who helped Colby make it to his bedroom for the night. At 11:25PM Colby was so drunk he could not walk a straight line. You escorted him to his bedroom, helped him take off his suit jacket and shoes. Colby plopped down onto the bed and passed out. You closed the door on your way out, but did not lock it.

Notice that when I give this part of the suspect sheet to the player that I have removed the notes (T) or (F) for True or False, so that none of the suspects can know what their guilt status is, based on their testimonies. This way they can not be sure which statements are factual or not.

Note that the examples here are cut straight from the suspect sheet,s but later we will write the Dossiers or 'safe' versions of the character sheets from which we will give them information.

Note: Don't forget that in my included scenario example that there are two crime scenes for the players to investigate. The players may establish the true scene of the crime and will want to investigate that area as well. You could either have a room or an area set up for it, or just hand the 'clues' out to the relevant suspects. The clues could be a prop, or an index card describing what they found, or both. The more elaborate you can make the investigation the more interesting and fun it will be for your players.

18c. The End

ACT#3

When time is up, or when the investigation and questioning has seemed to reach a dead end or a conclusion, announce that time has run out and the investigation stage is over. At this point the moderator can evaluate the situation, take votes, and then reveal the true solution to the game and the finale of the story. I will describe End Game variants in Chapter 23, which will help you determine a method for ending the game and evaluating the votes however you see fit.

For example, here are the Acts and Stages that should be played for Brenton Manor.

ACT ONE (The Beginning)

Stage#1 Before Dinner
- Guests arrive sometime afternoon, probably after lunch.
- Guests introduce themselves and get casually acquainted to each-other.
- Moderator explains which rooms in their home (or wherever) represent important areas relevant to the game. Gives them each a map if necessary.
- As Colby, moderator greets the guests and explains who will be sleeping where.
- Characters perform their objectives for Act One, Stage#1.

Stage#2 Dinner
- As Colby, moderator announces dinner.
- The guests meet in the dining room, have dinner, and continue getting more acquainted with each other.
- As Colby, the moderator reveals necessary information about Colby's character, persona, and

relation to each of the guests. Some general story plot could be revealed here as necessary. Certain characters may reveal some information about themselves that may be important to plot.

- Characters perform their objectives for Act One, Stage#2.
- Dinner will conclude and the party will move to the lounge for drinks and conversation.

Stage#3 After Dinner

- Guests are given time to interact with each other and Colby for a short duration. Certain plot information and character information might get revealed here.
- Characters perform their objectives for Act One, Stage#3.
- Colby and Guests eventually retire to their rooms for the night in a certain order to reveal plot.
- Moderator announces that the night passes and turns into morning.

ACT TWO (The Middle)

Stage#1 Introducing the Butler

- Moderator announces that the night passes and turns into morning.
- Moderator announces Colby's death and announces that some one killed him.
- Moderator gives private notes to each character revealing what events took place from their point of view during the night if necessary.
- Characters perform their objectives for Act Two, Stage#1. (if any)

Stage#2 The Body

- Moderator shows the suspects to the place of Colby's corpse.
- Moderator gives private notes to each character revealing what they may gather from the scene.
- Characters perform their objectives for Act Two, Stage#2 .
- Suspects may discover the actual scene of the crime and continue the investigation.

Stage#3 The Locked Door

- Moderator explains the door to Colby's Bedroom is locked.
- Characters perform their objectives for Act Two, Stage#3. (if any)

Stage#4 Scene of the Crime

- Moderator hands out the clues to the appropriate suspects.
- Characters perform their objectives for Act Two, Stage#4.

Stage#5 The Investigation

- Moderator announces that the game is afoot and that they may continue investigating the crime scene and questioning each other.
- Moderator plays referee if necessary and may answer certain questions privately as needed.
- Suspects are given a certain time limit to investigate, gather clues, evaluate evidence and question each-other. Maybe an hour.
- Characters perform their objectives for Act Two, Stage#5. These objectives are always going to be the same for the Investigation part of the murder mystery game. They are as follows:
    1. Use what you know about the others to remove yourself from suspicion.
    2. Find a way to reveal the Clues to Reveal during Questioning. This is your testimony.
    3. Try to conceal the Clues to Conceal during Questioning without lying. If you are confronted with evidence you may have no choice but to confess the entire truth.
- After the time limit has been reached or it seems the investigation is reaching some sort of a conclusion the moderator announces that time is up.

ACT THREE (The End)

Stage#1 Conclusions

- Characters perform their objectives for Act Three, Stage#1 (if any).
- Moderator announces the end of the game.

Stage#2 Votes

- Moderator hands out a Vote Sheet to each player and allows them to vote on who they think did it, how they did it, and why they did it. They may also vote on best costume and best acting also.

Stage#3 Solution

- Moderator reveals the real solution to the game. Perhaps each suspect player has a short confession to reach which starts with the innocents reading theirs first, followed by the liar, followed by the villain!

19. OBJECTIVES

In the creation of the Dossiers, we will create and write objectives for the players to perform during each Act and certain stages of the game. In the early part of the game, objectives will be written primarily as a way to create interaction between the characters and to reveal hints to potential sub plots that will help tell the story.

During the first Act, objectives will consist of actions and dialogues that might drop small ambiguous or vague hints that could be valuable later, but will mostly be used to reveal characters personalities and to perform functions which help guide the game along its course. These are not scripts, as the players are free to act out the action however they like and deliver the dialogue however they like. The objectives are there however to prompt them to reveal necessary information, to provide some amusing situations, and memorable interactions.

During the second Act of the game, objectives will contain more valuable information that will be delivered either through dialogue or an action. Now that we know what each character knows, or thinks they know, about the others and the clues that they must reveal and the clues that they must try to conceal, we can easily use that information to write some of the objectives for the characters at each Act and/or stage of the game.

We can also use what we know about how each character will act, and react, during the investigation of the crime scene, and during questioning, to also write some objectives for the characters during the middle Act and stages. If necessary we can also use objectives to tell the ending part of the final Act and stages as well. You will want to try to write at least four, but probably no more than eight, actions or objectives for characters to perform during each stage. That may not always be possible. It is possible that there could be a stage where no character can perform any objective or action.

How many objectives a character must perform per act, will depend on how many stages comprise each act. You can have as many objectives as you like. The objectives do not need to be written into the Story Teller's version of the Suspect Character sheets, but they must be present in the players Character Dossier sheets. In the next chapter I will discuss how to create the Character Dossiers, which will basically be the 'safe' versions of the suspect sheets you created for your reference.

Be sure to read over the objectives I assigned each players character to perform to get an idea of how to write objectives for your own mysteries.

20. CHARACTER DOSSIERS

Now we need to create the 'safe' versions of the Suspect Sheets, which will be called 'Dossiers'. The Dossiers will contain all of the information each player will need to know in order to play their character objectives out during each Act and Stage in the game. The Dossiers should also contain costume suggestions, props, and perhaps advice on how to role-play the character.

This is fairly easy to do if you have been creating the Suspect Sheets in a word processor. Using copy and paste you can transfer all the information from the Suspect Sheets into a new file which will be the 'safe' player character Dossier version.

In the Dossier version, edit out all of the 'dangerous' information from the Suspect Sheets and re-word things if necessary. Dangerous information would be any details that would indicate guilty, or not guilty status (i.e. Liar, Villain, Innocent). Remove any notes that would suggest their access to the weapon, motive, opportunity and make sure that they do not know which of their testimonies are true or false. Remove any information that would give away any secrets of the plot that the character could not know and any information the player should not know while playing their character.

Do not edit or overwrite the Suspect Sheets themselves, as we will still need those for our own reference.

Mind you that, when the game begins, you will not give the players all of their character information at one time. You will only give them certain sections of their Dossiers as needed, as it depends on which Act of the story you are 'directing'.

The first part of the character Dossier will contain a General Profile that will only consist of the essential information that the player will need to know when they arrive for the murder mystery party. When sending out the invitations to the players you will need to send them this General Profile for their character. The General Profile information should be as follows.

Name:

Gender:

Age:

Marital Status:

Occupation:

Areas of Expertise:

Political Affiliation:

Religion:

Hobbies:

Habits:

Costume Suggestion:

Props:

Acting Advice:

Relation to the Victim:

Relation to the other Suspects:

That should be everything the player should know in order to dress the part and play their character out during the game. Note that this information reveals who will be killed. If the victim is going to be alive when the players arrive you may also wish to add a notation that the crime has not been committed yet. Or just change 'Relation to Victim' to 'Relation to (name of victim)'. Here is what Madame Edwina's General Profile will look like when the player receives her invitation.

MADAME EDWINA
General Profile

<u>Name</u>: Madame Edwina (female) Age: 42

<u>Marital Status</u>: Married

<u>Occupation</u>: Psychic Consultant and Fortune Teller

Areas of Expertise: Insight, knowledge, matching fingerprint/handprint samples.

Political Affiliation: Un-affiliated

Religion: Metaphysical Spirituality

Hobbies: You study the Occult and perform Seance's.

Habits: Smoker and drinker.

Relation to the Victim: You were an acquaintance of Colby Brenton, he was fascinated with Astrology and Tarot and he often consulted with you for advice concerning love and money. Note that Colby Brenton will still be alive when you arrive for the murder mystery game.

Relations to Other Suspects: You are married to the Constable, Derryl Gramlich. The two of you have an unusual marriage. Derryl works a lot and you run a small Psychic Consultation business.

Costume Suggestions: Colorful gypsy and nomad style clothing or metaphysical apparel. Fancy costume jewelry, lots of make-up, a veil or fancy head-dress. Black boots and stockings.

Props: You smoke Clove cigarettes. You do not have to smoke a real cigarette, perhaps a fake one or a real one that is not even lit. Cigarette wand. Tarot Deck. Pack of cigarettes.

Acting Advice: You play a mysterious Fortune Teller and Palm Reader, perhaps you have a deck of Tarot cards handy in your purse. Your physical actions might be slow and languid. You are a quiet sort, listening to everyone else, before putting your two cents in about the spiritual, metaphysical, paranormal and occult aspects of any particular conversation. You like to mystify people with your words, your persona and style. You are a smoker and perhaps you have a cigarette wand. You always ask people about their Astrology sign like this;

"What is your Sign darling?"

This is all the information she will need before she arrives. There will still be more information in her Dossier, but she will not have access to it until it is time for each Act of the game to be played out. I discussed earlier about writing the Acts and Stages of the game, so here is what the rest of Madame Edwina's Dossier contains. When each Act is played she will only receive the information from her Dossier relevant to that Act.

For the most part, it is highly unlikely that any character should have any objectives or information to reveal during the final Act, unless you are going to have them read confessions after the vote.

Here is the rest of Madame Edwina's Dossier information. Notice how I used the information from the Suspect Sheet created earlier to deliver the information to her as it well be relevant during the game.

ACT ONE

STAGE ONE: Before Dinner

Objectives
- Introduce yourself to guests and ask their names.
- Find a guest willing to let you read their palm. Hold one of the subjects hands palm up in your left hand while tracing the lines of their palm with the index finger of your right hand. Use your imagination to improvise a fortune for them. Perhaps tell them they will come in to a great deal of money or will soon meet a new lover or that they have just experienced a long journey.
- Pretend to light up your cigarette and use your cigarette wand. Be flamboyant about this and pretend to blow your smoke high into the air. Perhaps you should be lounging in a chair or on a couch and have your legs crossed while doing this.
- Explain to guests that you are Colby Brenton's Psychic Advisor and Consultant. Whenever Colby has a question about love or money he consults you for advice.

STAGE TWO: Dinner

Objectives

- Wink at Colby Brenton.
- Complain about how much time your husband spends at work and how lonely you are sometimes.
- Ask Benita Lintner, the Maid, if she is from another country. Comment on her accent.
- Complain that your husband is a heavy sleeper and a snorer not to mention a bed hog.

STAGE THREE: After Dinner

Objectives

- At some point walk past and behind Colby while trailing a hand across his shoulders. Ask him how he has been doing lately, with a wink.
- Pretend to light up your cigarette and use your cigarette wand. Be flamboyant about this and pretend to blow your smoke high into the air. Perhaps you should be lounging in a chair or on a couch while doing this.
- Ask a guest if they would like to set up an appointment for an Astrology Reading sometime.
- Shuffle through your Tarot Cards, lay them out in a pattern consisting of five cards. Pretend to study them for awhile, then put the cards back into the deck.

ACT TWO

STAGE ONE: Introducing the Butler

No Objectives

STAGE TWO: The Body

Objectives

- Act horrified.
- You will notice Dust on the victims clothing, you will also notice it on the Maids outfit. You will bring it to the attention of the other suspects.
- You will find a broken pocket watch in Colby's pocket. The Story Teller will give this to you. It will read 12:45. Keep this information to yourself for now.
- Pretend to be disgusted by the sight of the corpse. Act faintish as if you are going to pass out. Sit down somewhere and fan yourself. Say you need fresh air and a glass of water.

STAGE THREE: The Locked Door

Objectives

- Suggest that the Maid would have access to the keys to the Manor.
- After the key has been located comment that Benita Lintner could be the culprit.

STAGE FOUR: Scene of the Crime

Objectives

- Sashay about the room languidly and look around.
- Comment that the room is a real mess.
- Comment that you feel Colby's spirit may be watching from the shadow realm.

STAGE FIVE: The Investigation

Objectives

- Use what you know about the others to remove yourself from suspicion.

- Find a way to reveal the Clues to Reveal during Questioning. This is your testimony.
- Try to conceal the Clues to Conceal during Questioning without lying. If you are confronted with evidence you may have no choice but to confess the entire truth.

What you know about the Others:

- Lisa Brenton (Dentist) had recently taken out an insurance policy on her husband, Colby Brenton. She would have gotten a lot of money if Colby were to die an untimely death.
- Colby Brenton was in some financial troubles and owed Lance Gibbins a lot of money.
- Benita Lintner (the Maid) was being blackmailed by Colby Brenton to work at the Manor for free, but you are not sure what dark secrets he was blackmailing her with.
- You claim Colby Brenton told you several times that he was afraid that his wife wanted to have him killed.

Clues to Reveal during Questioning:

- You claim to have been asleep in a guest bedroom with your husband. You may also claim to be very weak, tired and in poor health these days.
- If it is ever revealed you went to the Balcony for a smoke, shrug it off and just explain you forgot to mention it as it did not seem important to you.
- If someone asks you if you saw your husband take his sleeping pills, you will say yes.
- If someone suggests the ashes might match your peculiar brand of cigarettes you could say:

"Everyone knows that Colby smoked cigars. I am not the only one who smokes around here as you might have noticed. Those ashes could have come from the hearth for all we know."

- If it is pointed out that one of the lipstick smudges might match your brand of lipstick you will recall the other was on his collar when you went to visit Colby in his bed room. You will suggest the Beautician, Claire Ruppel, could shed some light on the matter.

Here is what you could say:

"How interesting, I would not have any idea on how that could have gotten there, how can we even be sure who those belong to? Perhaps they are from Lisa -they are married after all. They could suggest any woman present. Why don't we ask Claire the Beautician to sort this out, I am sure she has some experience in cosmetics."

- If given a chance to read the threat note found in the victims pocket, you can match a fingerprint on it to the fingerprint of your husbands hand, or you can just simply suggest the handwriting is familiar to you as that of your husbands.

Clues to Conceal during Questioning:

- You must try and deny any accusations that you were having an affair with Colby.
- If your husband tells you he knew about the affair, you will be forced to confess the truth, but state you hid this secret because you did not want your husband to find out. Once you have confessed to the affair you should shrug it off as if it is not so important as asking your husband to explain why he never confronted you about it, and furthermore why he was threatening Colby.
- You must try to hide the fact that you went out to the balcony for a smoke in the middle of the night. You are unsure the exact time.
- When you were smoking on the Balcony you saw a shadowy figure walking around in the garden, possibly a man. You can not reveal this until someone suggests you went to the Balcony for a smoke or you will be caught in a lie.

That ends all of the information which will be contained within Madame Edwina's Character Dossier, but as mentioned before she will only receive certain parts of it during each Act of the game. So, when creating each dossier, put each Act on a separate page or pages as needed. When it is time to play the game and you come to an Act, you would give each character that page from their Dossier for that particular Act. Then you would tell them which stage of the Act they are about to play and to complete only the objectives for that particular stage. Be sure to tell them that they do not need to read everything, but only that which is relevant to the current stage of the game.

Here are the other suspects Character Dossiers.

BENITA LINTNER

General Profile

Name: Benita Lintner (female) Age: 33

Occupation: Maid / House Keeper

Areas of Expertise: You can match dust samples and carpet fiber samples.

Political Affiliation: Un-affiliated.

Religion: Theist.

Marital Status: Single.

Hobbies: Does gambling count?

Habits: Light drinker, Social smoker.

Costume Suggestion: French Maid costume comes to mind. Black high heel shoes. A black short sleeved dress with short skirt. White thigh high stalking's or black fishnet panty-hose. A small white apron. A black bow in your hair. A choker or a white lace tied into a bow around your collar or a couple of gaudy fake plastic pearl necklaces. Wearing heavy red lipstick.

Props: A feather duster would be nice. Any cheap duster would work. You have a key, an old skeleton key would be great, hidden in your pocket.

Acting Advice: You are the sexy Maid. If you can do a sexy accent of some kind that would be fantastic. You are somewhat flirty. You are always noticing dust and cleaning it as you sashay around. Your body movements are fluid and sensual. You smile a lot. You tend to act a little bit ditzy. You do not always understand exactly what other people mean if the subject is rather complicated. You like to act innocent also. You are a casual smoker and drinker.

Relation to the Victim: You work for Colby Brenton at the Manor.

Relations to Other Suspects: You work for Lisa Brenton, the Dentist at the Manor. You would also be acquainted with Nelson Brenton, the Tobacconist.

ACT ONE

STAGE ONE: Before Dinner

Objectives

- Introduce yourself to guests and ask their names.
- Make it known that you are employed by the Brenton family. You have worked for them for a few years.
- Laugh or giggle at Erik Macha's jokes. You think they are funny or cute.
- Erik Macha will flirt with you, how you react is up to you.
- If Nelson Brenton makes a snide comment to you say 'Humph!' emphatically and walk away.
- Pretend to dust and tidy things up, organize thing, make them look nice.
- In front of the other guests ask Colby Brenton if you can speak to him in private before Dinner.
- Avoid the Banker. Tell him you are busy.

STAGE TWO: Dinner

Objectives

- If asked if you are from another Country tell her you are an American.
- If someone asks what you and Colby had a conversation about before dinner tell them it is none of their business and change the subject.

- Tell someone you work part time as a waitress for 'Teds Diner'.

- If someone asks about your hobbies tell them you like to gamble a little here and there.

- Try to avoid conversation with Lance Gibbins. You do not like him.

STAGE THREE: After Dinner

Objectives

- Avoid conversation with Lance Gibbins and Derryl Gramlich.

- Spend time hobnobbing with Erik Macha. Ask him about hobbies.

- Ask someone if you can bum a cigarette. Explain you rarely smoke.

ACT TWO

STAGE ONE: Introducing the Butler

Objectives

- Ask James, the Butler, why he was not able to make it to Dinner last night.

- Ask James how his family is doing.

STAGE TWO: The Body

Objectives

- Pretend to be sad and teary eyed. Ask someone for a tissue.

- Comment what a nice man Colby Brenton was.

- Hug Lisa Brenton.

- You will find the Dust Clue. The Story Teller will give this to you. You will suggest it is similar to the dust found in his room and that it does not seem to match the dust of the Billiard room.

- If questioned about the dust on your clothes you might say something like;

'So what about the dust? I'm the Maid, I clean and dust here all day, there are any number of ways I could have gotten this dust on me. The dust you see on Colby's clothing matches the dust found in his room. I do clean his room occasionally as well as you might imagine, it is my job after-all.'

STAGE THREE: The Locked Door

Objectives

- The Key will fall from your pocket. Take the key from your pocket and drop it on the floor but pretend you do not know how the key ever came into your possession.
- If questioned about the key you say something like:

'I do have access to all the keys of the Mansion, do I need remind you that I work here?'

STAGE FOUR: Scene of the Crime

Objectives

- Hold your hands to your face and gasp. Comment on what disarray the room is in.
- Suggest it looks like something very bad happened here in this room.
- You will look around the room and find a Bullet. The Story Teller will give this to you.
- You will show the Bullet Clue to the Constable.

STAGE FIVE: The Investigation

Objectives

- Use what you know about the others to remove yourself from suspicion.
- Find a way to reveal the Clues to Reveal during Questioning. This is your testimony.
- Try to conceal the Clues to Conceal during Questioning without lying. If you are confronted with evidence you may have no choice but to confess the entire truth.

What you know about the Others:

- Nelson Brenton, the Tobacconist, would have a reason to want Colby dead, as he would inherit the Estate and the Manor. You make it clear that you do not like him and suggest that he could be the culprit.
- You saw Madame Edwina, the Fortune Teller, smoking on the balcony while you were puttering around the Manor late at night.
- You saw Erik Macha, the Barber, coming inside the back door of the Manor from the garden sometime after Midnight. You also saw him hiding something suspicious in his room before dinner last night.
- Claire Ruppel, the Beautician, was embezzling money from the Estate trust accounts.

Clues to Reveal during Questioning:

- You will reveal that you were up late cleaning-up after the guests. You did not go to bed until sometime around 12:40 AM.
- Someone may ask why you were snooping around Colby's office. Turn away from them quickly and claim you were cleaning.
- If someone asks if Colby Brenton was Blackmailing you, the answer is No.
- If, and only if,someone asks you if you had an argument with Colby the day before, deny it was an argument.You did have a private conversation, but not an argument, Colby told you he had plans to end the affair with Madame Edwina, but try to keep this a secret as long as possible.
- If someone asks if you were taking bribes from Colby Brenton to keep quiet about his affairs, you will confess that it is true, and that you really needed the extra money. Colby is dead, there is no more point in covering for him anymore. You will act very embarrassed, hang your head down in shame, you will be very apologetic to Lisa Brenton, the Dentist, about this. You have felt guilty about this for a long time. You want to give Lisa a hug.

Clues to Conceal during Questioning:

- When snooping around Colby's office you were making sure Colby had not left out any information about your true identity that the Constable might find.
- You are not who you claim to be. Benita Lintner is not your real name. You are not only an illegal immigrant, but you are also wanted by Law Enforcement for Identity Theft Charges, Forgery, and Conning several men you dated out of large sums of money, which you squandered on gambling. Your real name is Evette Dupont. You do not want anyone to learn your true Identity. Colby found out about your real name and your true identity, but knew nothing of your darker secrets, other than your status as an illegal immigrant. If the Constable finds out who you really are you will be in a lot of trouble, and possibly be deported back to France, where you are wanted for even deeper darker secrets that you will never confess to.

LISA BRENTON

General Profile

Name: Lisa Brenton (female) Age: 32

Occupation: Dentist

Areas of Expertise: Matching teeth marks to bite wounds.

Political Affiliation: Democrat

Religion: Theist

Hobbies: Reading and Writing

Habits: Breath Mints, You are a casual drinker but you do not smoke.

Costume Suggestion: Medical Scrubs or perhaps a short sleeved white lab coat, or button up shirt. In your shirt pocket, a toothbrush, a dental mirror and light pen. A button or pin that has a picture of a tooth on it or a happy smile or the words 'Open Wide' on it.

Props: Breath Mints and Pill Bottle. Maybe Dental Floss and small tube of toothpaste.

Acting Advice: Despite how friendly and professional you are, nobody and I mean nobody, likes the Dentist. Probably because you are always lecturing people about brushing at least three times a day and flossing daily. You also bug people about their addictions to smoking and hard candies. You tell them its bad for their teeth and breath. As such, you are always self conscious about your own breath, and are addicted to breath mints. You are married to Colby Brenton. Your sister is Claire Ruppel the Beautician, the two of you have a sisterly love/hate relationship and you feel like she is always competing with you. You suffer from migraines and keep subscription medication with you for pain.

Relation to the Victim: You are Colby Brenton's Wife. You have been married four years.
Relations to Other Suspects: Claire Ruppel is your sister.

ACT ONE

Stage One: Before Dinner

Objectives

- Introduce yourself to guests and ask their names. Let them know you are Colby's wife.

- Nag people about proper Dental hygiene and all that sort of thing.

- You will notice that the Barber has a cavity and should come see you at your office as soon as possible.

- You will also nag the smokers about their smoking habits at least once.

- Hug your sister Claire Ruppel, then ask if she needs any help with money this month.

- If it seems the Banker, Lance Gibbins, has become upset and wants to leave ask him to please stay for Dinner.

- Reveal that you are friends with the Constable, Derryl Gramlich.

Stage Two: Dinner

Objectives

- Socialize with the Constable, Derryl Gramlich, he is your friend after-all, and you invited him to Dinner.
- Say that you feel as though you are getting a headache.
- Ask Benita Lintner if she finished all her cleaning duties for the day.
- Roll your eyes at Erik Macha's jokes. They were funny earlier, now they are getting on your nerves.
- Ask Lance Gibbins, the Banker, if his wife is a good cook.

Stage Three: After Dinner

Objectives

- Ignore your husband Colby Brenton.
- Thank Lance Gibbins for staying for Dinner, tell him he has had too much to drink and should stay the night in one of the guest rooms. Take his keys if you have to.
- Ask Lance Gibbins how that Root Canal is feeling.
- Announce that you have a migraine and that you are taking a pill and going to bed for the night.
- Thank everyone for coming. Give your sister Claire Ruppel a nice warm hug. Give your husband Colby a weak shallow hug, then pretend to go to a room. You must not come out until 'morning'.

ACT TWO

Stage One: Introducing the Butler

Objectives

- Greet the Butler and ask if he has all of his affairs in order.

Stage Two: The Body

Objectives

- Colby was your husband and you were having some marital issues, but you are upset with his passing nonetheless. Act upset.
- You will notice a very small amount of blood in the corner of the victims mouth. It is not enough blood to gather a sample. Keep this information to yourself for now.

Stage Three: The Locked Door

Objectives

- Pretend to look in your pockets for a key to the Door. Explain that Colby was the only one who had a copy of a key to his bedroom.
- When someone drops the Key Clue pick it up or the Story Teller will give this to you.
- Explain that the Key is the only copy you are aware of and ask why the Maid had it.
- Pretend to unlock the door.

Stage Four: Scene of the Crime

Objectives

- Ask Derryl Gramlich if he thinks this is the real scene of the crime.
- Pretend to look around the room searching for more clues. You will find the Pillow Clue.
- The Pillow has a minute amount of blood on it. It is not enough blood to gather a sample but

you will suggest that it could be the weapon used to murder Colby Brenton.

- When the Revolver is found, explain that you did not know that Colby was keeping a gun in the house and that you are afraid of guns.

Stage Five: The Investigation

Objectives

- Use what you know about the others to remove yourself from suspicion.
- Find a way to reveal the Clues to Reveal during Questioning. This is your testimony.
- Try to conceal the Clues to Conceal during Questioning without lying. If you are confronted with evidence you may have no choice but to confess the entire truth.

What you know about the Others:

- Your husband, Colby Brenton owed the Banker, Lance Gibbins, a great deal of money and he has been pestering Colby to pay up or face the consequences.
- The Maid, Benita Lintner, has no reason to murder anyone. She is very passive and kind to everyone. She might be a little secretive, but she is honest and loyal. She once cut her hair very short and donated it. A wig was made out of it and given to a young girl that had lost her hair.
- Erik Macha, the Barber, hated your husband, Colby Brenton, over differences in political views. You do not care much for Erik Macha but your husband did invite him, not you.
- Derryl Gramlich, the Constable, had absolutely no motive to kill your husband. When and if someone suggests he does have a motive, you will debate it until you discover the truth.

Clues to Reveal during Questioning:

- You claim to have been asleep in your room the entire night. You also claim that before going to bed you took a heavy duty pain killer for a migraine.
- You will admit that you and your husband have been separated for quite some time and

although you still live in the Manor you sleep in a separate room.

- If asked what marital issues you were having with Colby, you must reveal that his drinking and money problems were causing you both a lot of stress and heated arguments.
- If asked if you know, or knew, of any affairs Colby was having, you will become a little upset and admit that you often suspected him of cheating, but never had any proof.
- Defend Benita Lintner. You like her very much as she has been a loyal worker for you.
- It might be revealed that Colby was having another affair with someone very close to you. How you react is up to you.
- It may be revealed that the Maid was keeping secrets from you and will be apologetic. How you respond is up to you.

Clues to Conceal during Questioning:

- Colby is your second husband. You were married before and widowed.
- Your first husband of two years died under mysterious circumstances that will be revealed during the course of the scenario.
- You took out a large insurance policy on Colby Brenton a few months ago and would get a lot of money if Colby should suffer an untimely death. You want to conceal the insurance policy information.

CLAIRE RUPPEL

General Profile

Name: Claire Ruppel (female) Age: 29

Marital Status: Single

Occupation: Beautician / Hair Stylist

Areas of Expertise: You can match lipstick samples to cosmetic brands and match hair samples.

Political Affiliation: Democrat

Religion: Theist

Hobbies: You like to dance.

Habits: Chew bubble gum. Smoker. Casual drinker.

Relation to the Victim: You are (victim) Colby Brenton's sister-in-law.

Relations to Other Suspects: You are (Dentist) Lisa Brenton's sister.

Costume Suggestion: Glamorous apparel. Fashionable hairstyle. Classy but light make-up, except your lipstick which is heavy. Your nails are all painted a bright flashy color. Heavy Perfume. Perhaps an apron.

Props: You might carry a tote bag of fashion and cosmetic products. Perhaps a pair of scissors. A pack of cigarettes and a pack of chewing gum. A comb.

Acting Advice: You chew bubble gum and smoke cigarettes. You are fairly conservative but very friendly, polite and out-going. You are a conversationalist and enjoy socializing. You probably want to comment on the nice clothes and hair styles the other suspects have or perhaps you suggest someone should stop by your salon so you can give them a make-over or do something exciting for their hair.

ACT ONE

Stage One: Before Dinner

Objectives
- Introduce yourself to the other guests.
- Establish that you are Lisa Brenton's, sister. Keep in mind that you and your sister have a love/hate relationship. You feel like she is always competing against you to be more successful.
- Establish that Colby is your brother-in-law.
- Ask Erik Macha, if he cuts his own hair. Suggest he should come by your Salon for a hair cut.

- Say 'Hello' to Colby but you are going to be somewhat uncomfortable around him.

- Pretend to smoke a cigarette.

- Someone may ask you out on a date. Ask for details if so, then tell them you will have to think about it.

Stage Two: Dinner

Objectives

- You do not like Benita Lintner, the Maid, very much. Only small talk with her, if at all.

- You are still uncomfortable with Colby. Pretend nothing is wrong.

- Ask Nelson Brenton if he has had any dates lately. You used to date him. Tell him you might be able to set him up on a blind date with one of your friends from the salon where you work.

- You love to talk about cosmetics, make overs, and salon hairstyling products.

- Comment on Madame Edwina's make up. You like how she has done it. Tell her she looks nice for her age.

Stage Three: After Dinner

Objectives

- You chew bubble gum. Let everyone see that you are going to have some gum. Ask if anyone wants some.

- Ask the Maid to get you another glass of Champagne.

- Ask Nelson what he thinks about Erik Macha, the Barber, and if you should consider going out with Erik on a date or not.

- Colby might ask you a question. If so, act uncomfortable, and respond however you like.

- When Madame Edwina starts playing with her Tarot Cards, ask her what they mean.

ACT TWO

Stage One: Introducing the Butler

• Tell James Grantham, the Butler, you missed him at Dinner last night.

Stage Two: The Body

Objectives
• Gasp in surprise! You are shocked.
• Comfort Lisa and Nelson.
• You will discover two lipstick smudge clues. The Story Teller will give these to you. Save discussions of these clues for the investigation and questioning stage of the game.
• You will notice there are no physical bruises or markings on the body and suggest that Colby could have been poisoned.
• You will know when to ask Madame Edwina if she will be alright. Ask the Maid to fetch her a glass of water.

Stage Three: The Locked Door

Objectives
• No Objectives.

Stage Four: Scene of the Crime

Objectives
• Pretend to look for clues and assist the others. You will find nothing.
• Express your thoughts concerning the death of Colby Brenton.

Stage Five: The Investigation

Objectives

- Use what you know about the others to remove yourself from suspicion.
- Find a way to reveal the Clues to Reveal during Questioning. This is your testimony.
- Try to conceal the Clues to Conceal during Questioning without lying. If you are confronted with evidence you may have no choice but to confess the entire truth.

What you know about the Others:

- Nelson Brenton (the Tobacconist) has a motive. He is Colby Brenton's younger brother and would become a likely Heir to the Estate and the Manor.
- The Lipstick Smudges might match Lisa Brenton's particular brand of cosmetics. (Remember that she is Colby's wife and your sister.)
- You suggest that Benita Lintner, the Maid, was having an affair with Colby Brenton and that he was paying her for 'certain' favors. You will also suggest the lipstick smudges might match her brand of cosmetics.
- You claim you over-heard an vicious argument between Erik Macha (the Barber) and Colby Brenton (the victim) the day before around 4:45PM taking place in Colby Brenton's room. The door was closed so you can not be positive about what was said but it sounded like a very heated discussion involving money and embezzlement. This event took place before Dinner was served that night. You were walking by Colby's room, after using the bath room to freshen up, and were on your way downstairs to the Lounge. You saw Erik Macha leaving Colby's room later around 5:00 PM.

Clues to Reveal during Questioning:

- You will claim to have no real motive to commit the crime.
- You claim to have been in your room the entire night.
- You do not know who killed Colby.

- At some point you may have an opportunity to match a hair sample. It will match Lance Gibbins (the Bankers) hair color and length.

- You have always disliked Colby's Maid. You claim you have suspected her of stealing from the Manor several times and suggested it to Colby, but he ignored your accusations.

- You may be asked to match the lipstick smudge samples to cosmetics, but you are trying to avoid doing this. If forced to do so, one smudge is yours, the other is Edwina's.

- You may be asked if it is true that your sister Lisa Brenton was ever accused of killing her ex-husband. This has been a big hush-hush dirty secret in the family for a long time. The truth is, yes. Her ex-husband was murdered. He was suffocated with a pillow. Lisa Brenton was the prime suspect. Her ex-husband was extremely abusive. She was tried in court but there was a mistrial on lack of evidence. She was acquitted of the charges and the case was dropped.

Clues to Conceal during Questioning:

- You were having an affair with Colby. You do not want your sister to find out.

- You will want to avoid matching the lipstick smudge samples because you know one of them is yours and it will reveal your dark secret. You do not want to pin them wrongfully on anyone else either.

- You were the last person to see Colby alive before he was murdered. After your sister went to bed you went to visit Colby in his bedroom at about 11:45 PM. You intended to break off the affair but he was charming with his words and actions. One thing led to another and the two of you made out for awhile. You accidentally left a lipstick smudge on his collar. Colby was still drunk when you went to see him, and after the brief make out session he passed out and fell asleep.

ERIK MACHA

General Profile

Name: Erik Macha   (male)   Age: 35

Marital Status: Single

Occupation: Barber

Areas of Expertise: (you can match hair samples)

Political Affiliation: Libertarian

Religion: Agnostic

Hobbies: You read Sherlock Holmes stories.

Habits: Pipe smoker. Light drinker.

Relation to the Victim: Acquaintance. Colby Brenton came to your Shop to get his hair cut.

Relations to Other Suspects: You are a casual acquaintance of Lance Gibbins, the Banker, you cut his hair.

Costume Suggestion: Black Shoes, pin-striped pants, button-up dress vest over a white button-up shirt. Bow Tie. Heavy cologne. Perhaps a waist apron. A flat top derby.

Props: In your pocket, a comb, a pair of scissors maybe. A tobacco pipe.

Acting Advice: You are a slightly overweight but jovial character. Always happy, always laughing. You know how to strike up a conversation by asking a million questions about anything and everything. You like to get people talking about themselves. You have a few jokes to tell, most of them everyone has heard before, the rest are just not funny. You do not like to talk about politics or religion. You would rather discuss philosophy and current events. You like parties even if you do not care much for the host of a party. You are single and divorced, you came to the party hoping to meet some single women to flirt with and/or date. You smoke cigarettes and use Cocaine. You read Sherlock Holmes stories.

ACT ONE

Stage One: Before Dinner

Objectives

- Introduce yourself to the others.
- After you meet the Constable, tell Colby you need to go to your room for a few minutes. If you do not know where your room is yet, ask where you will be sleeping for the night. Stay in 'your room' for about two minutes, or so.
- Try to score a date with the Claire Ruppel, the Beautician.
- Try to score a date with the Benita Lintner, the Maid.
- The Constable makes you nervous, you do not want to talk to him very much.

Stage Two: Dinner

Objectives

- If asked why you came to the party, Colby insisted that you should come meet his single sister-in-law, Claire Ruppel.
- Explain that you have a lot of trouble sleeping in strange places. Ask Lisa or Nelson if the house is haunted.
- Flirt with Benita Lintner, the Maid. You really want her to like you.
- If you get a chance, bring up your favorite subject, Sherlock Holmes mysteries. Talk about 'Hound of the Baskerville's' and 'A Study in Scarlet'.

Stage Three: After Dinner

Objectives

- Pretend to smoke your pipe.
- Make casual conversation with Claire Ruppel.
- Give Benita Lintner lots of attention. Tell her she has a lovely accent. Lots of compliments.

- Pretend to be interested in what Madame Edwina is doing.

ACT TWO

Stage One: Introducing the Butler

Objectives

- No objectives.

Stage Two: The Body

Objectives

- Tell Nelson and Lisa that you are very sorry for their loss.
- You will suggest that it appears as though Colby was either choked, suffocated, or was poisoned. You will admit that you can not be certain.
- You will not find any clues yet.
- Exclaim that the killer must be caught and brought to justice!

Stage Three: The Locked Door

Objectives

- When Lisa drops the key ask her how she got it.

Stage Four: Scene of the Crime

Objectives

- You will search the room for clues. If there is a chair in the, room examine it. You will find a clue, a hair sample, the Story Teller will give this to you. Say nothing about it just yet.
- Comment on the other clues that the others find.

Stage Five: The Investigation

Objectives

• Use what you know about the others to remove yourself from suspicion.

• Find a way to reveal the Clues to Reveal during Questioning. This is your testimony.

• Try to conceal the Clues to Conceal during Questioning without lying. If you are confronted with evidence you may have no choice but to confess the entire truth.

What you know about the Others:

• Sometime after Midnight you decided to go outside for a Cigarette. As you left your room you were walking down the hall towards the staircase to the Foyer. You passed Colby Brenton's Office. The Door was half open and you saw Benita Lintner, the Maid, snooping around in the Desk as if she were searching for something. You decided it was not your business and said nothing.

• You know that Derryl Gramlich, the Constable, has been spying on Colby Brenton and carries a concealed revolver even when he is not on duty.

• Lance Gibbins, the Banker, told you that Colby Brenton owed him a lot of money and that he planned on getting that money back any way he had to.

• One of your customers told you that Lisa Brenton was having an affair with a much younger man.

Clues to Reveal during Questioning:

• You do not agree with Colby's political affiliations. Colby is a Republican who often made fun of you for being a Libertarian.

• You did not like Colby Brenton, but not enough to kill him.

• You may be asked to match a hair sample found in the Scenario. You have no issue with this and will do it gladly. It will match the hair of Lance Gibbins, the Banker.

- Someone will accuse you of having a heated argument with Colby Brenton in his room 'last night'. You will deny the event ever took place. You will suggest that the person is mistaken, and that it could have been Lance Gibbins, the Banker.

- You claim to have been in your bedroom most of the night.

- You did not sleep well during the night. In the middle of the night you went out to the garden for a smoke and to walk around. You do have an opportunity so you will be questioned about everything that happened when you went outside to the garden for a smoke. You know it was sometime after midnight. It was dark and stormy, but the rain had died down enough for you to make it to the Gazebo in the garden. You claim the reason you wanted to go outside was for fresh air and a nice smoke. You were having a lot of trouble sleeping in such a strange place. You may say you were reflecting about the conditions of your divorce. You saw someone smoking at the second floor Balcony, sometime after midnight, but you are not sure who it was. You think that whoever it, was may have been wearing a night gown, and perhaps it was a woman. You are not sure if the person saw you or not.

Clues to Conceal during Questioning:

- You really want to hide the fact that you brought some cocaine to the party, you did not realize a Constable would be present. You hid this in your room as soon as he arrived and you are nervous about it. You do not want anyone to look in your room under any circumstances. You also traffic Cocaine in the back part of your shop, if the word got out you could lose your business and perhaps go to jail.
(Fact: Cocaine use in the U.S.A. was outlawed in 1914.)

- You may be asked to reveal what you hid in your room and you will not want to do this.

- You will still be very nervous about the drugs hidden in your room.

DERRYL GRAMLICH

General Profile

Name: Derryl Gramlich (male) Age: 45

Marital Status: Married

Occupation: Constable

Areas of Expertise: You specialize in Ballistics. You can identify gun-shot residue. You can match bullets to fire-arms. You can identify gunshot wounds and match them to fire-arms.

Political Affiliation: Communist

Religion: Atheist

Hobbies: None

Habits: Pipe smoker. Trouble sleeping.

Relation to the Victim: Acquaintance.

Relations to Other Suspects: You are married to Madame Edwina, the Fortune Teller. You are friends with Lisa Brenton, the Dentist, she invited you and she is Colby's wife.

Costume Suggestion: You play an off-duty Constable but there is no reason why you might not show up to the party just after work. All blue suit and tie. A badge on your suit jacket. A black derby. Fake glasses.

Props: Pocket watch. Whistle necklace. A note book and pen in your pocket for taking notes. Toy Pistol, hidden somewhere on your person. A pill bottle.

Acting Advice: You are inquisitive and like to be in charge. You like to present yourself as an authority figure. You are all about law and order. You are the strong silent type, observing everyone and everything, and asking people questions when they say something peculiar. You do not like jokes. You are very serious about everything. You may walk around with your hands behind your back. You might respond to peoples comments with 'Interesting.' You like to take notes on peculiar information. When involved in conversation, you are the 'Just the facts Ma'am or Sir' kind of guy.

ACT ONE

Stage One: Before Dinner

Objectives

- Introduce yourself to others.

- Make it known that you are a Constable but you are off duty at this time.

- Complain about the smokers when they smoke.

- Tell your wife, Madame Edwina, she should quit smoking, when she smokes.

- Claim you are allergic to the cigarettes your wife smokes.

- Ask Colby what is for dinner tonight.

- Pretend to eye Erik Macha suspiciously. Keep an eye on him to see what he is up to.

Stage Two: Dinner

Objectives

- Ask Erik Macha why he came to dinner tonight.

- Ask Lance Gibbins why he came to dinner tonight.

- Ignore your wife mostly.

- Ask Benita Lintner, the Maid, what she talked about with Colby earlier.

- You are friends with Colby's wife, Lisa Brenton, the Dentist. You were invited by Lisa.

Stage Three: After Dinner

Objectives

- Thank Lisa Brenton for inviting you to dinner and tell her it was a great meal.

- Talk with Lance Gibbins, ask him what he thinks about the Maid.

- Ask Nelson Brenton if he is keeping his brother Colby out of trouble.

- Ask Erik Macha why he is acting so nervously.

- Tell Nelson Brenton that Colby has had too much to drink and should go sleep it off.

ACT TWO

Stage One: Introducing the Butler

Objectives
- No Objectives.

Stage Two: The Body

Objectives
- Examine the body. You suggest that it is most likely that Colby Brenton was suffocated to death, but you are not sure how.
- Examine Colby's right hand. You will find a 'Gunshot Residue' clue. The Story Teller will give this to you. Tell everyone that Colby has fired a revolver recently.
- Act like you are deep in thought as you look around the Billiards Room.
- Look for bullet holes in the walls. You will not find any.

Stage Three: The Locked Door

Objectives
- Ask James Grantham exactly where he was throughout the duration of the night.

Stage Four: Scene of the Crime

Objectives
- Search the room. You will find the Revolver clue. The Story Teller will give you this. Tell everyone that this is the gun that Colby fired recently.
- Search the walls for bullet holes. You will not find any.
- When the pillow is found, look up towards the ceiling. You will discover a bullet hole in the ceiling. Tell everyone what you see and announce that this proves that Colby's Bedroom is

the actual scene of the crime. Whoever killed Colby moved his body to the other room.

- If someone shows you a bullet clue, tell them that it would fit the Revolver you found.

Stage Five: The Investigation

Objectives

- Use what you know about the others to remove yourself from suspicion.
- Find a way to reveal the Clues to Reveal during Questioning. This is your testimony.
- Try to conceal the Clues to Conceal during Questioning without lying. If you are confronted with evidence you may have no choice but to confess the entire truth.

What you know about the Others:

- Lisa Brenton, the Dentist, was once accused of murdering her ex-husband, but she was never convicted in court. Her ex-husband was smothered to death with a pillow.
- Colby Brenton owed Lance Gibbins, the Banker, a lot of money and Lance Gibbins intended to sue him in court or take other drastic measures to collect on this debt.
- You saw Claire Ruppel, the Beautician, sneak into Colby Brenton's room on your way to your bedroom. You thought it was suspicious, but decided it was not your business.
- You claim you saw Colby Brenton and Benita Lintner, the Maid, having a private and hushed argument shortly before dinner and Colby slapped her hard across her face. You decided it was not your business and said nothing about it. You think it occurred around 4:35 PM.

Clues to Reveal during Questioning:

- You tend to try and keep people focused on their testimonies. If someone's testimony seems to be drifting off on a tangent, you interrupt and direct them back to the original subject.
- You claim you take medication which helps you sleep. You took one of these pills before retiring to your bedroom for the night.
- You claim to have slept through the entire night.

- You and Edwina were sharing a guest bedroom. As far as you know she was there all night.

- You keep a concealed pistol with you off duty in case of emergencies.

- Some one will claim Erik Macha hid something in his room. You want to know what it was.

- Some one will claim the Maid was snooping around Colby's office. You want to know why.

- Someone may suggest your wife was having an affair and you will try to cover for her.

Clues to Conceal during Questioning:

- You are secretly involved with the Communist Political Party and you do not want anyone to find out, as it could really hurt your career in law enforcement.

- Your wife was having an affair with Colby Brenton and you are very embarrassed about this because you feel this reflects poorly on your image as a man.

- You spied on your wife and Colby Brenton to establish that the affair was true.

- You do not want your wife to know that you know. You are hoping to work things out with her because you love her. You have never confronted her about it.

- You wrote a threat note to Colby Brenton demanding he end the affair, and that if he did not, you would make him suffer for it. You do not want anyone to know about this note for several reasons. The note would implicate you as the possible villain. The threat could get you in some trouble with the Constabulary Station, as it would be considered harassment.

- Someone may accuse you of having written a threat note to Colby Brenton, and you did.

- Someone will want to see your note book, at first you will use your position as an officer of the law to refuse to submitting your note book as evidence. You will use everything that you know about the others to misdirect the suspicion on you. If someone states that you are lying about something you will always respond with the following:

"I am an Officer of the Law and I do not lie! You have no authority to question my honesty."

LANCE GIBBINS

General Profile

Name: Lance Gibbins   (male)   Age: 55

Marital Status: Married

Occupation: Banker

Areas of Expertise: (you can match handwriting samples)

Political Affiliation: Freemason

Religion: Theist (Supreme Being)

Hobbies: You like to play the Stock Market.

Habits: You smoke cigars and drink.

Relation to the Victim: Acquaintance

Relations to Other Suspects: You are a casual acquaintance of the Barber, Erik Macha, he cuts your hair.

Costume Suggestion: Grey business suit and tie. Top Hat. Fake Glasses. Cloth handkerchief sticking out of jacket pocket. Tie Clip. Cufflinks. Class ring.

Props: Pocket watch. Pen. Cigar. Wall street journal. Cane.

Acting Advice: You smoke a Cigar. You are the very serious business man. Money and Politics are your favorite subjects. You keep track of the stock market. You have a cane for looks, but you walk just fine, it is more a symbol of authority than it is a crutch. You always act very professional and sophisticated. You look down on those who are poor or are unemployed.

ACT ONE

Stage One: Before Dinner

Objectives

- Introduce yourself to guests.

- Tell Colby Brenton that you came to discuss some business with him in private.

- Act impatient. You do not care much about the party at this moment.

- Pretend to smoke your cigar.

- Ask Derryl Gramlich if he is on duty.

- After you have a talk with Colby Brenton you will be upset and want to leave. Lisa Brenton will ask you to stay for dinner. You will agree and say that your wife can not cook anyhow.

Stage Two: Dinner

Objectives

- Ask Benita Lintner, the Maid, if she works anywhere else besides the Manor.

- Apologize to Lisa Brenton for making a scene earlier.

- If asked why you came to dinner, explain that you had some business to discuss with Colby.

- Ask Nelson Brenton if he carries your particular brand of cigars at his shop.

- Tell Claire that your wife loves her Salon, but she spends too much money there.

Stage Three: After Dinner

Objectives
- Pretend to light up and smoke a cigar.

- Tell Lisa Brenton that you have had too much to drink and ask if you may stay the night. She should say yes. Thank her for her kind generosity.

- Tell Nelson Brenton you think he has better business sense than his brother and that he should be the one handling the family estate.

ACT TWO

Stage One: Introducing the Butler

Objectives

• No Objectives.

Stage Two: The Body

Objectives

• Tell everyone that the body is beginning to smell and cover your nose and mouth with your handkerchief.

• Tell everyone that you are not a crime scene investigator, that you will stay out of the way.

• Tell Lisa and Nelson that you are truly sorry for their loss.

• Complain that you will probably never see your money now.

Stage Three: The Locked Door

Objectives

• No objectives.

Stage Four: Scene of the Crime

Objectives

• You will pretend to search the room.

• You will find an Ashes Clue on the bed sheets. The Story Teller will give this to you.

• Ask Madame Edwina to show everyone the broken pocket watch clue and reveal it's time.

Stage Five: The Investigation

Objectives

- Use what you know about the others to remove yourself from suspicion.
- Find a way to reveal the Clues to Reveal during Questioning. This is your testimony.
- Try to conceal the Clues to Conceal during Questioning without lying. If you are confronted with evidence you may have no choice but to confess the entire truth.

What you know about the Others:

- You saw Erik Macha, the Barber, hiding something in his room shortly after the Constable arrived.
- Erik Macha, the Barber, disliked Colby Brenton over differences of opinion concerning politics.
- Benita Lintner, the Maid, often cashed checks at your bank with a questionable Identity Card. You could never prove the document was false or had any reason to believe the checks were fraudulent. All of them cleared, however, you suspect she is not who she claims to be.
- Nelson Brenton, the Tobacconist, was embezzling money from the Estate trust accounts.

Clues to Reveal during Questioning:

- You claim to have been sleeping in your room the entire night.
- You will reveal that you have been invited to the party by Lisa Brenton but your reason for accepting the invitation was to discuss business with the Brenton family.
- You are a casual acquaintance of the Barber, Erik Macha, he cuts your hair.
- You may be asked if you had an argument with Colby in his bedroom before dinner last night. You will deny it was an argument and claim it was a business discussion.
- You may be asked to match the handwriting of a note to another suspects handwriting style and you will have no issue with this. If you are given the opportunity to observe the Constables note book, you will notice it matches the writing style on the note.

- Someone might try to match a clue to you and you will not resist.

Clues to Conceal during Questioning:

- Colby Brenton owed you a large amount of money. He has been avoiding paying you anything at all on his debt and you were tired of it, you came to the party with intentions of collecting the money by putting some pressure on Colby.

- You had an heated argument with Colby in his bedroom before dinner at around 4:45PM. The conversation lasted between ten and fifteen minutes at most.

- Someone may suggest that Colby owed you a lot of money and you will confirm that fact. If pressed on the matter you will be forced to admit that the discussion turned heated. Colby got mad and pushed you into the chair in his room. You will then state that this angered you, but that an altercation was not going to solve the matter. You then told Colby you would see him in Court to settle the debt. You left his room intending to leave for the night, but Lisa Brenton convinced you to stay for dinner and said that she would talk to Colby about paying up on the debt as soon as possible. This placated you and you decided to stay the remainder of the night.

NELSON BRENTON

General Profile

Name: Nelson Brenton (male) Age: 29

Marital Status: Divorced / Single

Occupation: Tobacconist

Areas of Expertise: (you can match tobacco and ash samples)

Political Affiliation: Democrat

Religion: Theist

Hobbies: You collect coins and stamps.

Habits: Pipe smoker. Light drinker.

Relation to the Victim: You are Colby Brenton's younger brother.

Relations to Other Suspects: You are Lisa Brenton's brother-in-law.

Costume Suggestion: Derby. White button up shirt. Button up dress vest. Bow tie. Black pants. Black dress shoes.

Props: A tobacco pipe.

Acting Advice: You smoke a pipe. You own a Pipe and Tobacco Shop where you sell various types of pipe tobacco, cigarettes, special cigarettes, cigars of all types, magazines, newspapers, tobacco pipes, cigarette wand's, snuff, chew, etc. You are talkative and chatty, making a sale is important to you. You enjoy wine and know a lot about it. You smile and nod a lot when people make comments to you. You are polite and kind. You wink and tip your hat to the ladies. You are a happy man, despite the fact that you have not yet met the woman of your dreams. When contemplating serious matters you often cross one arm across your chest and with your other hand, you stroke your chin and raise an eyebrow.

ACT ONE

STAGE ONE: Before Dinner

Objectives
- Introduce yourself to the other guests.
- Establish with guests your relation to Colby and Lisa.
- Pretend to smoke from your pipe.
- Ask Claire Ruppel how she is doing and how is business down at the Salon.
- Tell Colby to try not to drink too much tonight.
- Make a rude comment about Benita Lintner, the Maid. You do not care for her much.

- If no one else will, let Madame Edwina read your palm.

STAGE TWO: Dinner

Objectives

- Tell Benita Lintner, the Maid, that she should be working, not enjoying dinner with the rest of the guests.
- Ask Claire Ruppel if she has met anyone special.
- Ask Derryl Gramlich if he has been working on any exciting cases.
- Congratulate Colby on scoring that big Jazz gig he got.

STAGE THREE: After Dinner

Objectives

- Pretend to smoke from your pipe.
- Tell Benita Lintner, the Maid, to make sure all the guests are being tended to.
- Ask Erik Macha if something is wrong.
- Stay close to Colby Brenton, you realize he has had way too much to drink.

ACT TWO

STAGE ONE: Introducing the Butler

Objectives

- Tell everyone what a hard worker the Butler is and that you wish the Maid would work just as hard as he does.

STAGE TWO: The Body

Objectives

- You are upset.
- You decide to stay out of the way while the others investigate the body.
- After awhile, you will notice a piece of paper in the back pocket of your brother. You will take it and read it and then fold it up and place it in your vest pocket. You decide it is too personal to reveal what it says to everyone else and refuse to let anyone look at it. This is the Hand Written Letter clue, which the Story Teller will give to you.
- Pray that your brother finds peace in the after life and comfort Lisa.

STAGE THREE: The Locked Door

Objectives

- None.

STAGE FOUR: Scene of the Crime

Objectives

- You will look around and assist the others but you will not find anything interesting.

STAGE FIVE: The Investigation

Objectives

- Use what you know about the others to remove yourself from suspicion.
- Find a way to reveal the Clues to Reveal during Questioning. This is your testimony.
- Try to conceal the Clues to Conceal during Questioning without lying. If you are confronted with evidence you may have no choice but to confess the entire truth.

What you know about the Others:

- Derryl Gramlich, the Constable, is a Communist and has been hiding it for a long time.
- Madame Edwina has been visiting Colby Brenton at the Manor a lot lately. Sometimes late at night. She has stayed the night a few times.
- Benita Lintner, the Maid, is not who she claims to be. You will suggest that she is hiding something and could be the culprit.
- Claire Ruppel, the Beautician, had access to various poisons such as arsenic and cyanide.

Clues to Reveal during Questioning:

- You are not all about money at all. You feel the simpler things in life are much better than money.
- You enjoy Jazz music, and often went to see your brother perform at the local venues. You have always been supportive of his talents and dreams, but have always been disappointed about your brothers drinking problem and bad money management skills.
- You do not care much for the Maid, Benita Lintner, you always felt like she was hiding something.
- You claim to have been sleeping in your room all night.
- There is no point in denying that you are now the most likely heir to the Manor and the Estate, but you will claim you had no motive to kill your brother because Colby has squandered away a large portion of the family's money.
- Everyone will want to know why you are concealing the letter, and you will reassure them that it is very personal and the information it contains is very sensitive.
- You were one of the last people to see Colby alive, as you were the one who helped Colby make it to his bedroom for the night. At 11:25PM Colby was so drunk he could not walk a straight line. You escorted him to his bedroom, helped him take off his suit jacket and shoes. Colby plopped down on to the bed and passed out. You closed the door on your way out but, did not lock it.

<u>Clues to Conceal during Questioning</u>:

- The contents of the letter. You will not bring it up until someone starts making some interesting suggestions about the Constable. When this happens, give it to the Banker. Suggest to Lance that perhaps Madame Edwina should see it also.
- You knew your brother was a cheater and it disgusted you, but you said nothing to keep the peace in the family. You often argued with Colby about his lecherous activities.
- You do not like the Maid because she would not date you.

21. GAME VARIANTS

Here in this chapter I will discuss a few variants for playing your murder mystery game. Chose the method that suits the game style you wish to play. Most murder mystery games are played one of two ways, either they are played with sleuth type characters or they are played without sleuth's.

21a. Clean Versions

Some Murder Mystery dinner party events must be appropriate for conservative guests and/or younger audiences. These types of Murder Mysteries Parties are called 'Clean'. To do this you would need to create a Murder Mystery scenario from scratch and avoid using references to sex, affairs, alcohol use, and illegal drug use. You may have to leave out graphic descriptions of the murder, crime scene and other such details. You might be able to use a scenario you wrote already, if you are able to edit out 'controversial' details while still retaining the integrity of the story and game dynamics. This is not so much a variant of game play but a version of the game style you might wish to play.

21b. Suspects versus Suspects or Suspects double as Sleuth's

This is the game version that I have been describing in the guide so far and by the example, 'Murder at Brenton Manor'. In this variant the suspects will actually double as sleuth's, none of them know who the villain is, not even the villain themselves. Each suspect matches wits against the other suspects trying to collect clues, evaluate evidence and testimony in order to solve the crime, even if it means confessing to win. The suspects all have their own areas of expertise they can use to evaluate clues. Each suspect also has a number of objectives to complete during each stage of the game as the scenario unfolds and there is plenty of opportunity for interaction between suspects.

With the Suspects versus Suspects version, you will only need a Host (you), and as many guests to play each of the suspects. The moderator, or another person, could play additional non-suspect characters roles for the story if needed. For example, in 'Murder at Brenton Manor' the host could play the part of Colby Brenton up until the time he goes to bed. When it is announced the night has passed, the moderator would then change the costume up a bit and take on the role of James Grantham, the Butler, who will continue to carry out the story. You could have another person play these parts if you wish, but make sure they can not know who the liar or villain are and do not really know the guilt status of any of the suspects at all.

If this is the variant you wish to play, just use the Game Rules as described in Chapter 22. The game is concluded however the moderator sees fit, based on the methods described in Chapter 23.

21c. Sleuth's versus Suspects Variant #1

In this variant the suspects would not examine the crime scene or find clues. The suspects will still perform all of their objectives, but excluding those which involve finding or handling a clue, in most cases. The game is played almost exactly as described before, except the suspects do not match wits with each other, instead the sleuth's match wits against the suspects and try to determine which of them is guilty. The suspects do not question each other, instead they are questioned by the sleuth's.

The sleuth's will find the clues and try to make sense of the evidence by asking the appropriate suspects. It is possible certain suspects will still find and handle a clue, if it is relevant to the telling of the story. For the first part, or Act of the game, the sleuth's are mostly bystanders, taking notes and silently observing the scenario unfold until Act Two, when the Investigation actually begins.

At that point the sleuth's get to be more involved interacting with the suspects and become part of the scenario itself. However, there is less interaction between the suspects themselves from this point on, since the sleuth's are doing all of the footwork. It works best if each suspect is in a different room paired up with a sleuth, each of the sleuth's take turns, rotating from one suspect to another, questioning the suspects until game time runs out. Perhaps each sleuth is allowed to question each suspect for about seven and a half minutes. Sleuth's vote on who they think is guilty before the true villain is revealed and the game ends in a method of the hosts choosing as described in Chapter 23. The advantage of this particular variant is that the game and story scenario unfolds in a similar fashion to a murder mystery play. You could have, in groups, as many 'sleuth's' as you could possibly want.

With the Sleuth's versus Suspects version you will need a Host (you), as many guests needed to play suspects, and either half as many guests, or as many guests as the total number of suspects, to play as the sleuth's or detectives. Example: If you have 8 suspects than have 4-8 sleuth's. If this is the variant you wish to play, there are two versions of the player rules used, one for the suspects and one for the sleuth's, these rules are explained in Chapter 22. If you do use this variant, you may also want to write some simple sleuth character profiles up for the players who will be playing the detectives. See Chapter 24 for ideas on how to do this.

21d. Sleuth's versus Suspects Variant #2

If you wish the sleuth's to be involved from the very beginning of the game, it works best if the scenario played involves a murder which has already been committed before the sleuth's arrive. The suspects were already, in theory of the story, at the story location before the sleuth's arrive. The Moderator would give out some safe information about the victim to the sleuth's and perhaps a description of events that could have taken place up until the time the body was discovered.

The sleuth's would examine the body, find clues, and investigate the crime scene. It works best if each suspect is in a different room paired up with a sleuth. Sleuth's take turns, rotating from one suspect to another, questioning the suspects until game time runs out. Give the sleuth's a time limit to question each suspect, about seven and a half minutes at most. When they are done or time runs out, sleuth's vote on who they think is guilty before the true villain is revealed. The game ends in a method of the hosts choosing, based on the methods described in Chapter 23.

The disadvantage of running the game in this particular method is that the suspects are deprived of acting out all of their objectives that tell the story up until the point the body is discovered and makes for a much shorter game. The sleuth's would have the major responsibility of playing up their characters while suspects are questioned individually and little of this would get witnessed by the group as a whole.

If this is the variant you wish to play, just use the two sets of player game rules, one for sleuth's and one for suspects, described in Chapter 22. If you do use this variant, you may also want to write some simple sleuth character profiles up for the players who will be playing the detectives. See Chapter 24 for ideas on how to do this.

21e. Large Group Murder Mystery Variant (up to 100 players)

This would be done a lot like those interactive murder mystery plays. To do this you would basically play the Sleuth's versus Suspects Variant #1 as a method to play the game.

The setting for the scenario for this type of variant would have to be something very exciting in order to keep the audience interested in the play that they are about to watch.

The suspects would be played by performers or actors and would act out the scenario up until the point where the body is discovered. You would need to write a special script for this. The characters the actors would play would be written a little differently than the methods described in this guide. You would want suspect characters who are all stereotypical, over the top, larger than life and perhaps even a bit comical. They would not have to have any particular occupation or area of expertise in this type of game because they will not be trying to solve the case themselves.

The Sleuth's would be played by the audience in a large reception style dining room so the audience would be seated at different tables. Each table would be considered a team of sleuth's and each table would be presented, by the moderator, with a large envelop containing all the clues that are to be discovered at this point of the game.

The moderator in this type of event usually takes on the role of a Detective of some kind to keep the audience focused on the case and to guide them in the investigation.

Since time constraints would make it nearly impossible, or very dull, the audience would not really be able to question each of the suspects individually. Even as groups this would be difficult. So the next part of the play would have to be acted out. There would have to be a script written and performed in such a way so that all of the important dialogue and actions could be acted out and presented to the audience.

After this skit is performed, the moderator would hand out another envelope to each table of sleuth's containing the rest of the clues. Since the sleuth's would not know how to match clues to suspects, the clues used in this type of game would be vastly different. The clues would have to be something your average audience member could understand and evaluate using common sense, some reason, and perhaps some logic.

Usually the clues presented allow the audience to use deduction to narrow down the list of possible suspects. Only the killer, in this case, would be able to have access to the actual weapon, a valid motive, and a definite opportunity to commit the murder. Circumstantial evidence and red herring clues would also be presented in the mix of clues but the audience members would have to be able to eventually determine which clues are valid and which are not.

Basically the method for deduction and the elimination of the suspects would work out with the following formula.

The Clues would show that, if you have eight suspects, that six of eight of the suspects had access to the legitimate weapon used in the crime or six of eight of the suspects were capable of performing the method of murder whatever that may be.

The Clues would show that of the six remaining suspects that only four have legitimate motives and that the other suspects motives were nothing more than accusations based on false rumors, gossip, or straight out lies.

The Clues would show that of the remaining four suspects that only two had an actual opportunity to commit the crime.

This would leave two suspects remaining and the Clues would prove that out of these two remaining suspects that one has a better alibi than the other which then leaves one suspect with absolutely no alibi of any kind with access to the weapon and a valid motive.

After everything in the script has been acted out, each table, or team of sleuth's would be able to make a vote as a team. The moderator would collect these votes, end the game similar to the methods described in Chapter 23, then reveal the tally of the votes as described in Chapter 23a. In most cases though, it is suggested that the end of the play always ends with the villain being caught and brought to justice. This makes for a good ending no matter how you look at it and the audience leaves satisfied that justice has been done.

Some large group interactive murder mystery games, or plays, actually have it set up so that one of the members of the audience would become the victim, and in some cases the game is set up in such a way that even one of the members of the audience would turn out to be the murderer.

21f. One of the guests will be killed! Variant.

This variant works with any of the above variant methods. All you would need to do is make sure none of your players, whether they be suspects or sleuth's, know which of them is to be killed.

You would invite a guest to play the part of the intended victim and you would develop their general profile just as you would one of the suspects or sleuth's. They would be given pieces of their Dossier just like everyone else up until the point that they are killed. In the 'Murder at Brenton Manor' example, all I would need to do, as the Moderator, is to announce that night has passed. I would lead everyone to where the body is to be found and then announce which one of them has been killed.

The guest who has been killed will then pretend to be dead, as long as needed, until after all the clues from the body and from the location where the body is discovered are found. The player of the victim would not need to lay around playing dead the rest of the night either. The other option is to have them change costumes and take the part of the Butler.

Alternatively the player, for the remainder of the game, could put on some make up and perhaps a white sheet. They could play the ghost of the victim during the remainder of the game, following everyone around silently. This way they can remain a part of the evenings festivities.

Another thing that can be done here is that it could even be possible for the players to be allowed to question the ghost. The ghost would not be allowed to reveal the killer, they would not remember that part of their life, but they could be allowed to answer certain questions that would be relevant to the plot or story without giving it away who the killer is. The player playing the ghost would not be told who the killer is anyways.

This type of idea adds a little bit of a paranormal theme to the story and would be great for a Halloween murder mystery game variant. Perhaps you would also require your suspect or sleuth players to perform a mock seance in order to contact the player playing the ghost in order to question him or her.

There could be several types of variants based on a Halloween theme. Perhaps the murder mystery is not about identifying a murderer, but about identifying which suspect is a werewolf before the next full moon. Perhaps there is a victim and the clues seem to indicate that the victim was attacked and killed by a werewolf. There is no motive really in this type of kill other than blood lust, instinct, or hunger. The werewolf would have to have certain traits that would eventually make him or her identifiable as the werewolf, based on clues found over the stages of the game. The same could be done with a vampire.

22. HOW TO PLAY THE GAME / PLAYER RULES

When sending out the invitations to guests you may wish to include some information and rules on how they may play the game. That way they will have an understanding of what to expect and will have some general advice on solving the mystery. However, before sending out these rules, be sure to read Chapter 21 and decide which game variant you will want to play.

Note that there are two sets of rules, depending on which variation of the game you will be playing. The rules for Suspects doubling as Sleuth's differs from the rules for Sleuth's versus Suspects. They are similar but are worded differently to avoid confusion. Here are the examples of the rules with tips I would send to players when hosting the example murder mystery we have been discussing. You would only need to change the first sentence and last sentence of these rules to reflect your particular scenario.

22a. Suspects versus Suspects / Suspects double as Sleuth's Game Rules

Murder At Brenton Manor

You have been invited to a dinner party at Brenton Manor. Someone will be murdered. The killer could be you. Your fellow friends, family, and guests may be Suspects in the crime as well. One of the Suspects will be the true Villain, one will be a Liar, and the others will be innocent.

Suspects doubling as Sleuth's try to establish each-others relation to the Victim, who has a weapon, motive, and an opportunity to commit the crime.

Each Suspect will have testimony to give concerning themselves. Some of this information they may reveal and the rest they will try to conceal without lying. They may change the subject or dodge the question but they may not out-right lie. Unless asked the right questions they may or may not reveal any information as they see fit.

Each Suspect will also have four pieces of testimony to share concerning what they know or think they know about the other Suspects, however, each completely innocent Suspect will have one false piece of testimony amongst those. No one will know which is true or false at the start of the game. Perhaps you will use what you know about the others to incriminate them or to take the suspicion off of yourself. The choice is yours.

The Liar plays their personal information the same as the other Suspects, however, the testimony they share about the other Suspects will only contain one factual statement. The rest of their testimony about the others will be completely false or very misleading.

The Villain will also play their personal information the same as the other Suspects, however, half of the testimony they share about the others will be true and the other half will be false or misleading. If you turn out to be the Villain you may have to confess in order to solve the crime or perhaps you will try to get away with the perfect murder. The choice is yours.

Will you rise to the challenge and solve the Murder at Brenton Manor?

For playing the Sleuth's versus Suspects game variant there are two versions of the rules, one set you will send to the Sleuth's and one set to the suspects. Here are the two version of rules for this variant. You would only need to change the first sentence and last sentence of these rules to reflect your particular scenario.

22b. Sleuth's Game Rules

You have been invited to a dinner party at Brenton Manor. Someone will be murdered. Your fellow friends, family, and guests may be Suspects in the crime. One of the Suspects will be the true Villain, one will be a Liar, and the others will be completely innocent.

The Sleuth's will match wits with the Suspects in order to establish each Suspects relation to the Victim, who has a weapon, motive, and an opportunity to commit the crime.

Each Suspect will have testimony to give concerning themselves. Some of this information they may reveal and the rest they will try to conceal without lying. They may change the subject or dodge the question but they may not out-right lie. Unless asked the right questions they may or may not reveal any information as they see fit.

Each Suspect will also have four pieces of testimony to share concerning what they know or think they know about the other Suspects, however, each completely innocent Suspect will have one false piece of testimony amongst those. No one will know which is true or false at the start of the game.

The Liar plays their personal information the same as the other Suspects, however, the testimony they share about the other Suspects will only contain one factual statement. The rest of their testimony about the others will be completely false or very misleading.

The Villain will also play their personal information the same as the other Suspects, however, half of the testimony they share about the others will be true and the other half will be false or misleading.

Will you rise to the challenge and solve the Murder at Brenton Manor?

22c. Suspects Game Rules

You have been invited to a dinner party at Brenton Manor. Someone will be murdered. The killer could be you. Your fellow friends, family, and guests may be Suspects in the crime as well. One of the Suspects will be the true Villain, one will be a Liar, and the others will be innocent.

The Sleuth's will try to establish the Suspects relation to the Victim, who has a weapon, motive, and an opportunity to commit the crime.

Each Suspect will have testimony to give concerning themselves. Some of this information they may reveal and the rest they will try to conceal without lying. They may change the subject or dodge the question but they may not outright lie. Unless asked the right questions they may or may not reveal any information as they see fit.

Each Suspect will also have four pieces of testimony to share concerning what they know or think they know about the other Suspects, however, each completely innocent Suspect will have one false piece of testimony amongst those. No one will know which is true or false at the start of the game. Perhaps you will use what you know about the others to incriminate them or to take the suspicion off of yourself. The choice is yours.

The Liar plays their personal information the same as the other Suspects, however, the testimony they share about the other Suspects will only contain one factual statement. The rest of their testimony about the others will be completely false or very misleading.

The Villain will also play their personal information the same as the other Suspects, however, half of the testimony they share about the others will be true and the other half will be false or misleading.

Will you rise to the challenge and help solve the Murder at Brenton Manor?

23. END GAME VARIANTS AND VOTES

Ending the game can be just as fun as playing the rest of the game and there are a number of ways this can be done, but it is always done after the players have had their time limit to evaluate clues and gather testimony. In my games I always let the players know that they are only allowed to make suggestions or theories of suspicions, but never are they allowed to make an official accusation during the game.

Their official and final accusation will be done when they make their vote at the end of the questioning round of the game. For each Murder Mystery Scenario I host, I always rotate the method for how I will end the game and reveal the solution so that my players will never quite know what to expect and to keep the last Act of the game feeling fresh.

Before we reveal the solution, however, we should let everyone fill out a vote card. The vote card should be something like this:

Your Real Name: (not the name of the character they are playing)

Whodunit?   (this where they write the name of the person they think is guilty)

How?   (this is where they would write the weapon or method of the crime)

Why?   (this is where they will write their theory of the motive)

Best Actor?   (so they can vote on who they thought played their character best)

Best Costume?   (so they can vote on who had the best costume)

There is always a vote to preceed the revelation of the final solution but each method for ending the game is a little different and each ending has it's own unique dramatical effect. So, first take the votes, but do not reveal the tally yet, than end the game with one of the following methods. After I discuss the variants for ending the game, Chapter 23a describes how to reveal the tally of the votes, because that should be done a certain way also. Here are a few game ending variants I usually choose from. You could write your own style of variant also if you desire.

The Confession Ending

What you can do is write a short confession for each of the suspects to read (maybe two paragraphs long at most) and they will read them in a certain order. The first confession to be read is prompted by the host and each confession ends with a keyword or name that prompts the next person to read their confession. The next to last person to read their confession will be the liar followed by the villain, who then reads their confession and reveals themselves as the murderer.

Each of the innocents who read a confession will reveal any dark and dirty secrets they were hiding plus any other relevant information they were trying to conceal followed by their admission for a motive if they indeed had a legitimate motive. After they have read that, they will state 'But I did not kill (the victims name). Perhaps it was (the next suspects name to read their confession).

This could make for a long ending for the game depending on how many suspects you have, so the alternative is to just write a short confession for each of the prime suspects to read in order. What I mean by 'prime suspects' is that they are the ones who seemed to really look the most guilty out of all the suspects in the scenario.

Perhaps just have about three of your suspects read a confession, this will include the liar who will read their confession just before the villain. So, have one innocent suspect read a 'confession' followed by the liar followed by the villain. This will keep the guests on their toes wondering which of them will have to read a confession next, and if they do not know you are going to end the game in this manner, at first they will think the first person asked to read a confession was the killer. This will, at first, make them think they were wrong about their vote if they did not vote for the person reading a 'confession'.

You should also end the liars confession with something like, 'I was the liar, but I did not kill (the victims name). Perhaps it was (the villains name). The villains confession would be the longest, as they would detail exactly how and why they killed the victim. Note the information I wrote for

Madame Edwina, the 'How you did it' part. All of that information would be included in her particular confession, rewritten from her viewpoint, so everyone would completely understand the events that led to the death of the victim.

After that has been done, reveal the tally of the votes as described in Chapter 23a.

The Alternate Ending

Or the 'That's how it could have been done. But how about this?' ending.
Done in the style for the endings of the comedy murder mystery movie, named after the popular board game by the same name, this ending is also a lot of fun.

This is done similar to the 'Confession Ending' except each confession will detail a possible but fake admission for guilt in the murder. The moderator writes three confessions total for the end of the game. The first person to read their 'confession' will be an totally innocent suspect revealing an false scenario of how they killed the victim and an admission of guilt for the murder except that their confession will end with the sentence, 'That is how it could have been done. But what if it was (the liars name)?'

Then the liar will also read a completely bogus confession the same way but ending with the sentence, 'The end? That is how it could have been done, but what if it was (the villains name)?

The villain reads their true confession of guilt in the scenario, including how they really did it, and ends with the sentence 'And that is what really happened!'

After that has been done reveal the tally of the votes as described in Chapter 24a.

The Elimination Ending

Another great ending for the game done in the style of a murder mystery play in which you will eliminate the innocent in a particular fashion.

After everyone has cast their vote the moderator asks everyone to stand in a row similar to a police lineup. The moderator would then hand everyone a note that reveals what access they had to either the weapon, motive, and/or opportunity. Remember that in the 'Murder at Brenton Manor' example scenario that those who had legitimate although unprovable alibis would not have an opportunity and thus not have access to the weapon used either. Everyone in the scenario seemed to have a motive, but remember that some of those motives were not entirely true. You would give them a sheet of paper that reveals what was in fact true in their particular case.

The moderator would then ask everyone without access to the weapon to please sit down. This would leave a few suspects still standing. Then the moderator would ask everyone without an opportunity to commit the crime to please sit down. This should leave one suspect standing. The Villain! If not than ask everyone without a valid motive to sit down. That should do it. Then have a confession ready for the villain to read explaining exactly how they did it and why.

After that has been done reveal the tally of the votes as described in Chapter 23a.

The Smoking Gun Clue Ending

This variant ending is not always an option, but in the 'Murder at Brenton Manor' example it is actually possible. After taking the votes you would have the liar read a confession admitting that they were in fact the liar, but innocent of murder. After that the moderator will give Lisa Brenton, the Dentist, the smoking gun clue in the form of a short skit that she will act out revealing that she has figured out who the murderer really is. She would reveal that she has come to a theory that Colby must have bitten his assailant.

She would explain how she came to this conclusion based on her observations regarding the blood on the pillow and the blood on the victims mouth. Then she would suggest that whoever has a bite mark on their person, probably their arm, is the villain. At this point the moderator would reveal that there is only one person who has this bite mark, Madame Edwina, the Fortune Teller, on her left arm. Madame Edwina now reads her confession detailing how she did it and why.

But what if the player in the role of Lisa Brenton, the Dentist, voted wrong? It does not matter. Lisa Brenton is solving the crime...not the player in the role of the Dentist.

After that has been done reveal the tally of the votes as described in Chapter 23a.

23a. VOTES

The outcome of the game does not always have to rely entirely on the suspects intuition and crime solving skills to be won. The real point of these games is to have fun. Everyone really wins if they played their character out to the best of their abilities and had fun doing so. This is why a voting system is the best way to reveal who was right and who was wrong. This is also why we most likely never want the suspects to know what their guilt status is, that way everyone can vote and even vote on themselves if they think they are guilty.

In the Sleuth's versus Suspects version, only the sleuth's could vote on a killer because the suspects themselves are not able to question each other during the questioning stage of the game. Which seems quite unfair because none of them can win the 'Solved the Murder at Brenton Manor' award certificate.

But they can still win either best costume or best actor if we tell the sleuth players that they must vote for a suspect when it comes to best actor and best costume. Likewise the suspects are still allowed to vote but not on who they think the villain is, instead they will vote on which sleuth will win best actor and which sleuth will win best costume. This way there are two winners for best costume and two winners for best actor. Then explain that everyone really won if they had a good time playing the game.

Perhaps after all the votes are tallied, before revealing who was right and who was wrong, have all the suspects stand together as they would at the end of a play. Ask the sleuth players to give them all a round of applause for doing a fine job and for making the game possible. This gives the suspects a chance for glory and an opportunity to bow.

Now you would tally the votes and reveal the results.

If no one voted for the killer than you could reveal that no one was right and that the killer escaped justice, even though the villain may have read a confession earlier. You would explain that although the victim confessed the suspects and or sleuth's did not produce enough evidence to make an arrest and procure a conviction. The villain will escape justice and remain at large.

If the majority of the tally of votes accuse an innocent suspect, you could explain that this suspect was blamed for the crime. You could then ask these players to discuss why they came to this conclusion. If none of the voters were correct in identifying the killer, you would then explain that the suspects or sleuth's gathered enough evidence and clues to make an arrest but that the accused suspect was found innocent in court and that the real killer escaped justice and remains at large.

If one or more person was correct, you could reveal the true killer was identified by them and announce them as the winners of the game. Announce that they have enough evidence to make an arrest or a citizens arrest and will be able to procure a conviction in court. This can be acted out if desired. The correct players could, perhaps, use a pair of fake plastic handcuffs and cuff the suspect while reading them their Miranda rights. Also have these winners explain how they came to the correct solution to the game. Another option is that you could allow the villain to, perhaps, pretend to commit suicide in order to escape justice.

Thats pretty much it for the game. All you would do now is announce who won best actor and best costume and hand out the certificates to the winners of the game.

At this point you are just about ready to host and play the sample game scenario, Murder at Brenton Manor, or perhaps you are ready to host and play your own scenario.

If you are going to play the Sleuth's versus Suspects variant of the game, perhaps you still need to write up some sleuth characters for your detective players to play. Simple methods for writing sleuth characters are explained in chapter 24.

When everything is completed, all there is left to do is to decide which of your friends or family should play each of the characters and send out the invitations. In a game where the Suspects double as Sleuth's, the writer of the game obviously could not play the part as one of the suspects because they already know who is and who is not guilty. The writer of the game could, however, play one of the suspects in the variant of Sleuth's versus Suspects so long as the writer can keep secrets.

If you do play a suspect, you must remember to remind the players that any of the suspects could be the villain, just because you are the moderator does not mean you are in fact the villain. You would perhaps need a way to decide randomly which suspect character you would play in order to make this fair because you would not want them to automatically think you are playing an innocent suspect either and eliminate you as a possible suspect right away. Sadly the writer of the game can never play a sleuth.

Before we send out those invitations, lets cover some advice on how to host and direct a murder mystery dinner party game. If you need sleuth characters move to the next chapter, if not skip to Chapter 25.

24. SLEUTH CHARACTERS

If you decide to play the game variant, Sleuth's versus Suspects, you may want to write up some simple detective type characters for the sleuth's to play. None of them will really have an area of expertise to use in solving the crime and they will rely on using the suspects as their personal crime scene investigation 'experts'. Here are some sample classic examples of stereotypical detective types from the murder mystery genre. By using these, you will provide your sleuth players an opportunity to have just as much fun playing a role as the suspects would.

24a. The Bumbling Inspector

Chief Inspector Cleaseau from the Pink Panther series would be a perfect example. This type of sleuth character could provide a little bit of humor, perhaps some colorful or clever jokes, and provide some comedy relief. These types of sleuth's in fiction usually solve their cases through a series of accidental and comical revelations which allow them to crack the case quite by mistake.

24b. The Hard Boiled Detective

Sam Spade and Philip Marlowe would be perfect examples of this type of sleuth character. These types of detectives are tough, cocky, cool, and rather flippant in their persona's and methods. They are the 'larger than life' stereotypes of the mystery genre, usually coming from a background where they live in a cruel and unforgiving world. These are the 'Just the facts, Ma'am' type of characters that could care less what your personal problems are. They usually rely on choosing between the lesser of two evils in their methods when solving a case.

24c. The Dilettante Detective

Agatha Christie's character Miss Marple and Jessica Fletcher would be perfect examples of this type of sleuth character. This is the amateur 'detective' character who is not actually involved in the law enforcement profession. They usually have an occupation that might involve them in scenarios where a crime has been committed and the real investigators are lost. They are usually mystery writers, journalists, investigative reporters, etcetera, who end up involved in the murder mystery by being in the wrong place at the wrong time. Using their insight and clever tactics they solve the case through luck, common sense, and general problem solving skills.

24d. The Classic Private Investigator

Sherlock Holmes, of course, would be the perfect example for this type of sleuth character. Using the classical methods of deduction they solve crimes using an extraordinary amount of keen observational abilities to establish peculiar information about the suspects in question and use logic and reason to evaluate clues and evidence. They gather clues from witness testimony by asking loaded questions which force the suspect to reveal the information they need.

24e. The 'Incompetent' Lieutenant

Columbo is the perfect example of such a sleuth character, who is not incompetent at all, but pretends to be an ignorant buffoon. Using this method the sleuth attempts to lure the suspects into a false sense of security so that they will underestimate the sleuth's crime solving abilities and hopefully make a critical mistake covering their tracks. This way the sleuth can catch them red handed. This type of sleuth also likes to act as annoying as possible in order to get under the suspects skin. They do a lot of double-talk and ask a lot of loaded questions in order to get the information they might need, and there is always the 'Just one more thing' or 'Just one last question'.

There are plenty of other examples of sleuth character types you could use, feel free to do some research, or base your detective characters on your personal favorites in the genre. You can gather inspiration from games, movies, books, or perhaps even from real life. It is up to you.

25. HOSTING YOUR MURDER MYSTERY DINNER PARTY GAME

Make some invitations to send out to your guests. You will want them to RSVP, so be sure to note that on the invitation as well as your address, phone number, date, time, and a map to your home if needed. You can buy invitations, or make your own.

Send out your invitations at least five to six weeks ahead of time. You want to be sure that everyone has time to make arrangements and plans to attend your party. Real life can rear it's ugly head unexpectedly, so the more notice you can give the better, but you also do not want to plan so far ahead that your guests will forget to mark their calender. Keep in touch with them to see if anything has come up that might keep them from attending. You may also want to confirm with them one last time a week prior to your event just in case. If someone is unsure if they can be available or not, you may need time to ask a neighbor or another friend to fill in for that character.

Let your guests know how much time you intend to spend playing the murder mystery scenario on game night and make sure they have no obligations that might require them to leave early. You could play a murder mystery game in a single afternoon or evening, an entire day, or even as an entire weekend event. The more time you intend to spend hosting your murder mystery event may depend on planning and hosting other types of activities as well to keep guests entertained and to fill in gaps of times between certain events which comprise your actual murder mystery game scenario. Treasure hunt style games, location based mystery quiz games, scavenger hunts and other types of games might work just fine.

Always keep a backup copy of all the character Dossiers in case of an emergency. Your guests may lose them or forget to bring them.

Always have a back up plan. The success of a Murder Mystery Dinner Party can never be pre-determined. What if one of your suspects is sick at the last moment and can not attend? It could be nearly impossible to replace them on short notice. Be sure to have some other form of entertainment ready for the guests who do show up. A 'Treasure Hunt' game is a great backup plan, because they are not dependant on any number of participants, and your guests will still feel as though they got to partake in some sort of mystery and that they did not dress up in costume for nothing. Alternatively, a popular tabletop board game, of a similar theme, and an old mystery movie could work just fine also. With any luck, everyone will understand, and perhaps be able to reschedule the game for another night.

Only invite friends or family who are dependable. You want to invite guests that you know are really enthused and interested in playing such a game. You want to invite the ones who will not mind dropping their inhibitions for a few hours and forgetting about real life to take on the role of the characters which you have assigned them.

You may consider asking a few other friends to be on standby as replacements, but the draw back to this is that they may wonder why they are not being invited to have an active part in your party to begin with. A solution to this, is to invite someone to your party who will play non-suspect characters. That way, if someone falls out on game night, you can ask them to play the absent suspect character. You could then fill in for the role of the non-suspect character that person was going to play.

If you can, try to match the characters to each of your guests based upon their persona's. You can probably make a fair guess who would be able to play off each character best and who will be at ease playing particular parts.

Let players know it is okay to ad-lib their characters, so long as it does not conflict with the story line of the scenario. For example, you do not want to allow any one of your players to try and tell you that their character has some unique skill, or crime solving ability which will give them some sort of advantage in the game, or over the other players. They may develop their character, but not make them into a super hero crime solving genius. They must rely on their own wits, the area of expertise assigned to them by their occupation, the available evidence and testimony in order to try and solve the case.

Let your guests know that the characters you have assigned them are 'Top Secret' and that they are not allowed to reveal any information to anyone until the game begins. If you are playing the game with costumes it will probably be somewhat difficult for your guests to keep their part entirely secret, and that is okay, so long as they do not discuss any of their characters personal information everything will be fine. This is part of the reason we do not want to share all of their characters information with them before game night. The less they know, the less they can accidentally let slip out in conversation with their friends, family, and spouses.

As guests arrive, give them any introductory character information and game materials they may need. Give them a name tag to wear with their characters name and characters occupation on it. This will avoid confusion later and keep players from having to keep asking who is who over and over again during the game.

You could supply your players with a little notebook and a pencil in order to take notes. Perhaps have a card set out as a reference listing each suspects name and occupation. You could have another card set out with the 'safe' general information about the game scenario and victim notes for reference. You can get all this at a dollar store for cheap.

Stay confident and keep everyone focused on the story. As the host and moderator, you must be willing to keep the game running smoothly and take authority when necessary to remind the guests to stay in character. The point of the game is to solve a murder mystery, not chatting about television shows and that new movie that just came out. Perhaps as guests are arriving, give them some time to get small talk and general chitchat out of the way. When the game begins social hour is over.

If you are providing dinner for your guests, choose a meal that suits the needs of your game, party, and story. If an elaborate dinner suits your needs that is fine, but remember that you are already providing a great deal of entertainment and will be doing a lot of work as the host and moderator. Perhaps pizza, or a simple finger food buffet style meal will work the best in most cases, as it can be hard to host a dinner, and this type of game at exactly the same time. Preparation and cleanup of a fancy dinner may only complicate your evening and the primary focus of the evenings fun. A finger food potluck is also a great dinner idea for game night, as everyone would be contributing to the meal and drinks.

Use wise judgment when serving alcoholic beverages. You may want to limit the amount you have available on game night. A little social lubrication is fine and helps lower your players inhibitions enough to play their characters, but too much can really ruin the whole party real fast, and leave you with further complications. You do not want to have to fight someone for their car keys, call a cab for them, or escort them to a guest room to sleep it off for the night, and the last thing you want is someone to get ill.

If you are having the costume variety of murder mystery dinner party, perhaps you can give out special prizes for best costume, best performance, and perhaps award certificates for those who were correct in solving the case. You want all of your players and participants to feel appreciated for playing in your game. Send 'thank you' cards later, and perhaps a copy of the story you wrote as a token to remember the occasion. All of this will keep them wanting to play another one of your fabulous murder mystery games. You can find blank award certificate templates online to use.

You can also use paint shop to create vote sheets for use in your games. Vote sheets should ask who is accused of the crime, how they did it, and why. You might also want to include a space for voting best actor and who wore the best costume. Be sure to also have a space on the vote sheet where the player writes their real life name, so you will know who voted for who.

After the game, or as guests arrive, be sure to get some photos taken. You will probably want to save these pictures for the memories for years to come, and to show off to potential players for another mystery you have yet to write or host. There is no better way to get people interested in your events than by showing off pictures of your guests in their costumes, holding props, and having a great time at your event.

In Chapters 27 and 28 you will find suggestions for costumes, props, and decorations for your event.

26 DIRECTING THE GAME ON GAME NIGHT

By using the story line notes and the time line notes you should have, by now, been able to put together a number of Acts and game stages that must be played out in order to tell the story. As the moderator, directing the game is quite different than how the players will play the game. Once again, I will have to use 'Murder at Brenton Manor' as an example here, because I can not know the specifics of the game scenario you will write, so all I can do is show you exactly how I would host this example scenario. By reading this example, you should be able to determine exactly how to direct, and host your own murder mystery scenario game.

Step#1 As guests arrive, I allow them to get general chitchat out of the way and perhaps let them introduce their characters to each other.

Step#2 After all the guests have arrived, I announce that the game is starting.

Step#3 I read the player game rules to the guests and ask if any of them have any questions. I answer their questions to the best of my ability and then move on to the next step.

Step#4 I read them the introduction to the story. The introduction story for 'Murder at Brenton Manor' is as follows:

It is the Roaring Twenties, August tenth, Nineteen Twenty Two, to be exact, and you have been invited to Brenton Manor to attend a special dinner celebration for a Mister Colby Brenton. Colby Brenton is the current owner and heir to the Brenton family estate and resides here with his wife and younger brother.

Other guests have been invited to attend this special event as well. Please join us for this special occasion where you will meet new and exciting people, some of which you may already know, and experience an evening of mystery and entertainment.

Before we get started I would like to introduce you to Colby Brenton, our host for this evenings entertainment.

Step#5 Playing the part of Colby Brenton, I introduced myself to the guests and introduced the other guests to my wife, Lisa Brenton, and my younger brother, Nelson Brenton.

Step#6 I now announce that we are beginning Act One, Stage One and hand out these Acts from the Dossiers to the appropriate players. I will explain that they only need to read the information for Act One, Stage One: Before Dinner.

Step#7 I will announce that Act One has begun and that the players may perform their objectives for Stage One. Since the first Act takes place in a common room, such as a Lounge, I do not need to move the game to another location.

Step#8 Playing the part of Colby Brenton, I also perform any objectives for his character, as needed for this stage of Act One. I had to take Benita Lintner, the Maid, into a bedroom for awhile, as we had to pretend to have a brief private discussion. When we came back I also had to take Lance Gibbins to a room for a few minutes, for another pretend brief private discussion.

Step#9 After the conversations and actions have died down, I announce the end of Stage One.

Step#10 Playing the part of Colby Brenton, I will pretend to explain to the guests that this is an over night event, and pretend to show them which rooms they will be sleeping in. I give them access to a map which represents the layout of the Manor.

Step#11 After doing this, I announce that we are moving on to Act One, Stage Two.

Step#13 As Colby, I announce that Dinner is ready and direct guests to the Dining Room.

Step#13 I allow everyone to get food and drinks and to get seated at the Dinner table.

Step#14 After all guests are seated, I tell the players that they may review their objectives for Act One, Stage Two. After they appear to be ready, I tell them that they may now perform their objectives for this stage of the game.

Step#15 Playing the role of Colby, I also perform his objectives. One of which describes exactly why everyone has been invited. Colby is celebrating the fact that he just scored a big gig at a popular local venue and that his music career is just now starting to really take off in a positive direction.

Step#16 After the conversations and actions have died out, I will see to it that everyone has had enough to eat, before moving the game on to Act One, Stage Three.

Step#17 I announce that we are moving back to the 'Lounge' for after dinner drinks and conversation.

Step#18 After everyone has convened in the 'Lounge', I announce that we are beginning Act One, Stage Three and tell the guests that they may now perform their objectives for this stage.

Step#19 As Colby, I also perform Colby's objectives for this part of the game.

Step#20 After the conversations and actions have died out, in the role of Colby, I announce that the evenings entertainment has come to an end and that everyone will be retiring to their rooms for the evening. As Moderator, I prompt the guests to go to their rooms in a certain order and prompt those players to perform the actions relevant to this.

Step#21 I prompt Lisa Brenton to go to bed first, and ask her (as Colby) why she is doing so.

Step#22 As Moderator, I explain that Colby has become very intoxicated and that Nelson must help him to his room for the evening. I also act this out with him.

Step#23 I will then explain the rest of the guests have also retired to their rooms. Then I ask a rhetorical question, 'Or did they?'

Step#24 As Moderator, I explain that as the night passes that it was a dark and stormy night.

Step#25 As Moderator, I explain that night has passed and that it is now morning. Then I explain that we have ended Act One and that we are moving on to Act Two.

Step#26 I go to a private room and change out of my Colby Brenton costume and put on my costume for James Grantham, the Butler.

Step#27 Before I hand out the Acts to the players for Act Two, I will introduce myself as the Butler.

Step#28 Now I hand out the Dossier information to players for Act Two, and tell them they need only read the objectives for Act Two, Stage One. I will also explain that only a few characters have some objectives to perform for this particular stage.

Step#29 As the Butler, I perform my objectives and interactions with the other players.

Step#20 By now, I have announced the death of Colby Brenton, as it was part of the Butlers objectives to do so. I read an introduction for Act Two as follows:

(In a fake snobby posh English accent...)

Good morning Ladies and Gentleman, I am James Grantham, the Butler. First, I would like to thank you all for coming to Colby Brenton's celebration party and I do apologize that I could not be here to join you for last nights festivities as I had been detained by some rather important personal matters. I also regret to inform you that our host, Mister Colby Brenton, has passed during the evening. May he rest in peace. Let us have a moment of silence in his honor.

(I let everyone gasp and what not)

Yes, Colby Brenton is no longer with us, I found his body when I came in to work this morning. I found Colby's remains in the Billiard Room, so if you will please follow me I would like to show you exactly as I found him, so that you may witness for yourselves the unusual circumstances of his death.

(I lead everyone to the 'Billiards Room')

As you can see, there is something very peculiar afoot at Brenton Manor. I have been able to determine that Mister Brenton has not died of any natural causes and while I can not be positive exactly how he was killed, I can for a fact announce that one of you murdered him some time during the passing of the night.

(I let everyone gasp and what not)

Yes, one of you murdered him, and before I call the proper authorities, I suggest that whichever of you is guilty, either confess now or we will all be forced to investigate the matter ourselves to determine which of you is the Villain.

(no one knows if they are guilty or not so there should be silence)

No one wants to confess to their heinous crime I see. Very well, I am determined that we can find out how Colby was killed and why, but first we must determine which of us is in fact innocent or guilty based upon the available evidence. After-all, we do not want to accuse the innocent until after all of the evidence has been thoroughly examined, and we have all given our personal testimonies. By then, we should be able to determine which of us, is in fact guilty.

Step#21 As Moderator I announce that we are on Act Two, Stage Two and that everyone may now perform their objectives for Stage Two. I also hand out the clues and describe where and how they were found.

Step#22 Everyone has received their clues for this round and are able to try and evaluate said clues to the best of their abilities. By now, hopefully, the Constable has been able to determine that the location of the body is not the actual crime scene itself. If not, as the Butler, I prompt the Constable to discover what he must in order to come to this conclusion.

Step#23 I give the players some time to discuss where the actual crime scene could really be. If they do not come to a conclusion on this matter, as the Butler, I suggest the following:

Perhaps the murder was committed in Mister Colby Brenton's Bedroom, as it seems all of the clues so far indicate that Colby was most likely killed while he slept. Therefore, it would seem logical to investigate the master bed room first, before wasting a lot of time scouring the rest of the Manor for clues, which we might not ever find, all things considered.

Step#24 As the Butler, I lead them to 'Colby's Bedroom' and explain that the door is locked.

Step#25 I now announce that we are on Act Two, Stage Three and tell the players to perform their objectives for this stage. Only a few of them do and it does not take long.

Step#26 A real key was used as a prop, so I did not need to hand a clue card representing a key to Benita Lintner or to Lisa Brenton.

Step#27 I gave the guests a few moments to consider what just happened, and then explain that Lisa Brenton was able to unlock the door, using the key.

Step#28 As the Butler, I lead everyone inside the bed room and announce that everyone should perform their objectives for Act Two, Stage Four.

Step#29 After all clues have been distributed, the actions and dialogue have died down, I announce the game is afoot and that everyone should now move onto Act Two, Stage Five.

Step#30 I announce that the players have precisely one hour to perform an investigation and question each other, but that they are not allowed to make any actual accusations until the time of the vote. I explain they may suggest nothing more than possible theories and general suggestions, but to save their final accusations for the voting round of the game. I tell everyone they must also try to accomplish their objectives for Act Two, Stage Five before time runs out.

Step#31 After time has expired, or it seems the investigation has come to a dead end, I announce that time has run out and that we will move on to Act Three.

Step#32 There were no objectives for any of the players to complete for Act Three at all, so I explain that the final Act involves a conclusion, and a possible solution to the game events.

Step#33 I handed out all of the blank vote sheets and told everyone they may vote for whoever they think is guilty even if they think they themselves are in fact the villain. I also direct them to vote for best costume and best actor of the evening.

Step#34 After the votes were finished, I collected the Votes and made a private record of the results.

Step#35 I ended the game as described in Chapter 23, and used the Alternate Ending variation to reveal the true solution to the scenario. In my event only three people were correct, so I allowed them to pretend to arrest Madame Edwina, the Fortune Teller. As they did so, as the Butler, I said the following, to wrap up my part as James Grantham.

So Madame Edwina, you were the killer after all, what a terrible shame that you should have sunk so low in character as to kill Mister Colby Brenton, for simply ending an affair that should never have occurred in the first place. I do hope you find peace, and some sort of reconciliation for your crimes while you spend the rest of your life behind bars.

Step#36 I only announced who was correct and awarded them their certificates, followed by handing out the certificates for best actor, and best costume.

Step#37 I announced the end of the game and thanked everyone for coming.

Thats it. Using the above example, you should have a pretty good idea on how to host and direct your own murder mystery dinner party game. Have fun. In the next two chapters, I give advice for costumes, props, and decorations for your event.

27. CHARACTER COSTUMES AND PROPS

Your guests need not spend a lot of money on their costumes and props for their characters. Perhaps they already have an old dress or suit in their closet collecting dust that could be used, or modified, to make a costume. Old prom dresses, bridesmaid gowns, etc. They might be able to put something together from clothes or apparel that they already have in their wardrobes. Maybe they can borrow the clothes from someone they know.

Another idea is to hit yard sales or thrift stores. A lot of unusual clothing can be found at a decent price at second hand stores. If your players really want to raise the bar, they may opt to buy a costume from a costume store, or perhaps even rent one. Almost any type of costume or prop imaginable could also be ordered off of the Internet. Thrift stores, dollar stores, and second hand stores are also great places to find character props at a decent price. If they can not find something in particular, perhaps they can make their own props somehow, with regular household junk items.

The Costumes do not have to be 100% authentic or perfect, let your guests use their personal creativity to come up with a costume if they so desire, because if nothing else it will make that character they are playing all that more memorable when all is said and done. Sometimes, an old hat, a feather boa, fake plastic pearl necklaces, fake plastic glasses and an old jacket might do the trick just fine for those who are limited on funds.

If one of your players characters are to bring a prop, such as a gun or some other type of weapon, be sure to tell them they are only allowed to bring a toy, or a safe representation of the item. Never use, or suggest the use of, real weapons of any kind in your games. I would not even suggest realistic replicas, but I will leave that to your discretion, and perhaps you should warn the other guests that replicas of weapons may be present during your game night.

28. GAME PROPS AND DECORATIONS

There are several ways of creating simple and affordable props to serve as clues or decorations for you murder mystery parties. Decorating your home for game night, need not be expensive either. Here are some suggestions for setting the mood with simple and affordable decorations.

Set the atmosphere, you may have one or more rooms set up to represent important areas in your game's story. You can use whatever props you like to decorate. They do not have to be perfect. For example, I do not have a pool table to put in a room to represent the Billiard's Room for my story example, so I expect my guests to use their imaginations. The real decor of the room is irrelevant. The only thing you must do, is to describe what the room looks like as it is relevant to the story.

You could hang signs on, or above, the doors in your homes to label rooms like 'The Study' or 'The Billiards Room' or any other type of description you might need.

You could have props serve to represent only those details which are most important to the story, or use no props at all, and rely entirely on the imaginations of your guests. You could set a mood and atmosphere in your home with candles or night lights and low overall lighting. The less your guests can see in your mundane rooms, the more they will be forced to use their imaginations. You do not want it so dark, however, that someone could become hurt by tripping over some unseen object. Safety first. Your entire home does not need to be decorated to do this, just the actual rooms or areas you will use to play the game.

Hide or replace those family photos hanging on the wall with printouts of vintage photos or art appropriate to your theme and genre.

Hide those objects or appliances in your home that would ruin the theme and genre of your story. When hosting 'Murder at Brenton Manor', the theme is the Roaring Twenties, so I hid the television with a fancy lace shawl. You could use a sheet, cloth, or blankets to do this also.

You do not need to create a play house or movie set for your ambience, there are plenty of cheap decorations you can buy from a party store that well set a mood just fine. For the Twenties theme, I used black and white balloons and ribbons to decorate, as well as some old movie posters I found on the Internet and printed them out. Be creative and use your imagination.

For a body, you could make a dummy, by stuffing old clothes with newspaper or straw or whatever you might have available. Piece the dummy together and lay it out as the corpse for your victim. Perhaps you have access to a mannequin, or some other type of dummy. If your body must be bloody for you story, you can make fake blood with cherry drink mix, just use a lot of the powder and mix it with a little bit of water until you have the consistency that you desire. You can buy fake blood around Halloween time at dollar stores or chain stores, if you like, or just use a juice or a wine that you know will stain the color you desire. Pour or paint the blood on the body where you think it should go. No one has to be a blood spatter expert.

Another simple option is to place various pillows on the floor, in such a way as that when it is covered with a white sheet, it appears as though a body is underneath. The victim has been covered with the sheet during the investigation out of respect perhaps. Set your clues here for more decor.

You do not even need to have a body. You could use chalk or tape and make a 'victim outline' on the ground or floor where the body was found, just like in the movies. Place your clues that will be found in this area in the appropriate places. Maybe even use some yellow ribbon to mark the area off.

To make clues like a hair sample, perhaps you have a long hair cat, and you brush it with a special brush. You can take that hair off the brush, glue it to an index card and place it at the crime scene to represent the clue. Be imaginative creating props for your clues. A lipstick smudge on a shirt collar or napkin is easy enough to pull off...provided you have some makeup handy. Borrow your wife's. But ask first. Creating a gunshot residue clue could probably be hard to do, but you could just spread some clear clue on the hand of your dummy and then sprinkle it with pepper. If it's a chalk outline just make a note of this clue on an index card and place it on the hand area of the outline.

In those crime scene photos, you often see numbered marker cards on, or near, the chalk outline. You can do the same thing, just place numbered index cards where they should be at the crime scene, and then provide a list of clues matching what each number represents. Simpler yet, you could just provide each suspect or sleuth with a piece of paper with a drawing of the victim outline on it, and let them examine it for a moment. The diagram would possibly list each clue and where it was found on the diagram, then just hand out index cards, describing each clue, to the appropriate suspects. They can then read the clue to themselves and make a note of what it might mean to them.

You can always use the Web to get theme party decoration ideas. You can also add ambience with music appropriate for the theme and genre of your story. For my story example, some classic Big Band style Jazz music would be great. You can also put together a sound-track of music on CD to play. Need some theme music for your game for free? I highly recommend you check out incompetech.com where independent music composer Kevin MacLeod has made numerous mp3's FREE to download in a variety of different genres and styles. All of his music is professionally scored and fantastic to listen to.

Sometimes, burning some incense in your home can give it some added ambience as well. Using potpourri or boiling scented oils can work just as well. Adding a pleasant aroma to a mundane environment can really help the atmosphere feel unique and exciting.

You can be as easy and cheap as you like, or as elaborate as you desire. The more interesting you make your game, the more likely your players will remain interested and involved in your game. You want to make it exciting for them, give them an experience they could not normally have in real life. Make them feel as if they are part of a real play, or a movie, if you can.

Some hosts may wish to go so far as decorating even the outside of their homes as well for game night. This could be done with paper bag lights along the path leading up to the front door of the house to create a warm inviting welcome for the guests to come. Perhaps hang strands of tiny white party lights or Christmas lights along the front of your home. They could be draped around bushes or wrapped around trees. They could be trailed along the edges of porch railing or along the edge of your fence. Props, such as signs, and cardboard cutout silhouettes of items relating to your genre could be placed outside as well.

Once again, thrift stores, dollar stores, yard sales, your attic, your basement, your shed, might hold a treasure trove of possible items you could use as decorations or props for your game. Setting up the game in this way can be some work, but you will probably not even notice it, as it is a lot of fun to let your creative side run free as you decorate your home for your fabulous murder mystery. You may be able to find a ton of ideas for decorations and props, simply by looking it up on the Internet. The Internet is your friend.

Last but not least, and as mentioned before, but worth mentioning one last time...
Never use real fire arms as props, always use toy's to represent these, even if they are unloaded, it is just a really bad idea. It is probably a good idea, to only use fake weapons as props. Some guests might get nervous about the presence of actual weapons. Use your own discretion. The best thing to do is, for example, if you must use a real lead pipe as a prop for a weapon, is to set it wherever it will be discovered, but do not allow anyone to touch it or to pick it up, instead, hand them a clue card that will represent that item for the duration of the game.

This concludes the guide. I do hope you found this guide to be useful and I hope you have a great time creating, writing, and hosting the murder mystery dinner party games of your dreams.

<u>NOTES</u>